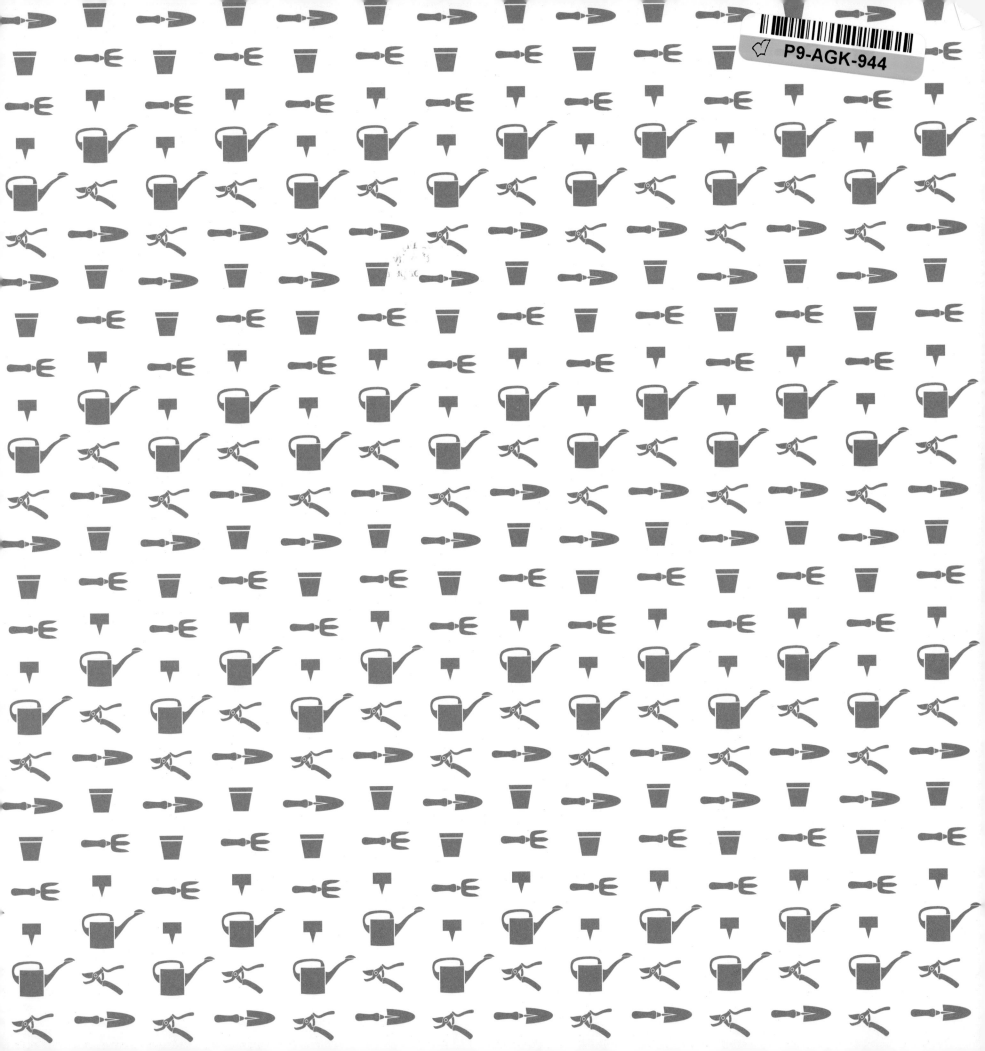

Start to plant

CONTAINER GARDENS

Create your ideal garden with these simple-to-follow projects

Graham A. Pavey

CHARTWELL BOOKS, INC.

A QUINTET BOOK

Published by Chartwell Books
A Division of Book Sales, Inc.
114 Northfield Avenue
Edison, New Jersey 00837

This edition produced for sale in the U.S.A., its territories and dependencies only.

ISBN 0-7858-0368-8

This book was designed and produced by
Quintet Publishing Limited
6 Blundell Street
London N7 9BH

Creative Director: Richard Dewing
Designer: James Lawrence
Project Editor: Diana Steedman
Editor: Janet Swarbrick
Photographer: Keith Waterton

Typeset in Great Britain by
Central Southern Typesetters, Eastbourne
Manufactured by Bright Arts (Singapore) Pte Ltd
Printed by Leefung-Asco Printers Ltd, China

Author's Acknowledgments

I would like to give special thanks to my wife, Chris; and to Maureen Cattlin, Ian, Mike, Ray, Mags and all the staff at Milton Ernest Garden Centre, Milton Ernest, Beds., U.K.; and Steve Woods and the staff at Tacchi's Garden Scene, Huntingdon, Cambs., U.K.

Picture Credits

The Publisher would like to thank the following for providing photographs and for permission to reproduce copyright material.

Graham A. Pavey: *pp. 8, 12, 16, 20, 25, 30, 32;*
Richard Key: *pp. 7;*
Garden Matters: *pp. 17, 18, 21, 24, 27, 35, 36.*

Contents

INTRODUCTION

No garden is complete without carefully placed ornaments and planted containers, and where space is limited, such as on a balcony or in a tiny backyard, containers may form the complete garden. Professionally planted flowers, herbs, fruit, and vegetables overflowing from pots and tubs, cascading from hanging baskets and swelling window boxes look stunning – but can they be achieved by the layman? The answer is YES, as long as some simple rules are followed and a sound aftercare regime is pursued.

This book will show how, with a little know-how, some forethought, and care, it is possible to create impressive container plantings that will enhance the whole garden. The secret is in the preparation, choice of plants, attention to feeding, watering, and caring for your new garden feature.

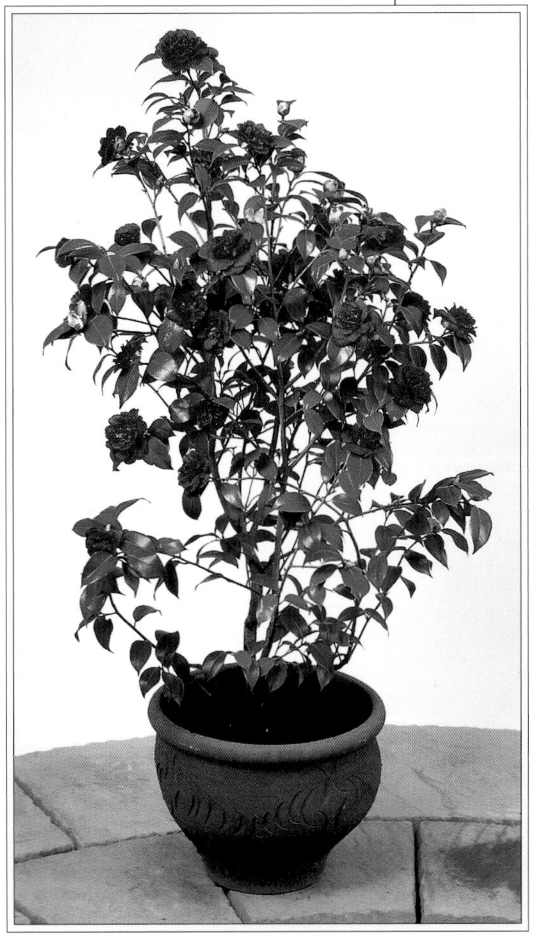

Most smaller containers are mobile and can easily be moved to anywhere in the garden, but it is important to position large permanent containers in the right place. Their positioning in the garden can be critical – for instance, a well-placed empty flowerpot can look more attractive than an award-winning container of moisture- and shade-loving plants that have dried up in drought conditions in full sun.

We explore the best ways to use containers in the garden, the different types of containers, and the tools, materials, and techniques required for planting them up and aftercare of your plants. Nineteen easy-to-follow projects are described with clear instructions on how to get the best from your container plants.

MATERIALS AND TECHNIQUES

Containers are available in a wide range of shapes, sizes, and materials.

Containers

Terra-cotta is probably the best choice of material for pots and containers. It is kind to plants, retaining moisture and keeping the roots cool, and looks good in most garden styles and especially on warm patios. In temperate climates, it is important to choose the best quality pots, because poorly fired terra-cotta is not frost hardy, and will crack in a severe or prolonged frost.

Concrete is usually seen in the form of classical containers and urns, useful in historical recreations or large country houses. Care should be taken in a small garden where an inappropriate design may look a little incongruous.

Plastic copies of terra-cotta and lead containers are difficult to distinguish from the real thing, and the advantage is that plastic is a light material – ideal for roof or balcony gardens. The disadvantage of plastic containers is that the soil in them dries out more quickly and they do not weather as well. If you use other types of plastic containers, remember that the container should not be the focus of attention, but rather it should be used to show off the plants, so choose a subdued color. Many are a bright white, and these can be dealt with by painting dark green.

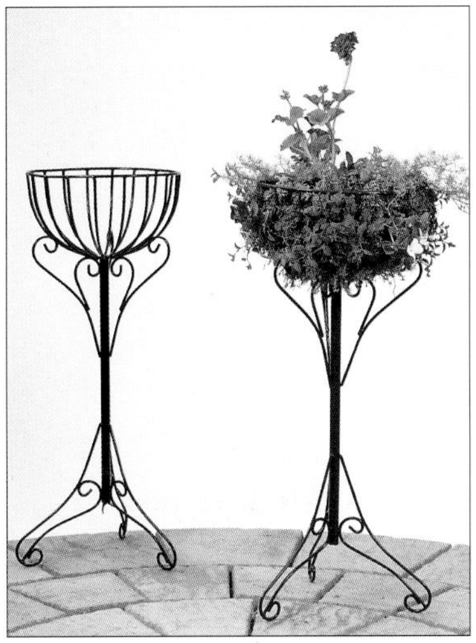

Free-standing and hanging baskets made from plastic-coated wire and painted cast iron.

Wooden containers, which come in many different types, from the traditional Versailles tub to a wooden barrel cut in half, need careful placing. They may not be suitable for some locations – in a country garden or on a farmhouse porch are, perhaps, the most appropriate.

Metal containers of all kinds can be used as long as they can hold soil. Lead urns and containers are a good choice for a period garden. Those available are mainly antique, but good copies are now commercially available.

Glazed pots and containers are available in a variety of shapes and sizes, often with an oriental design. Use them with caution because too bold a pattern on their side will detract from the plants.

Plants for glazed containers must be chosen with care. This Japanese maple, Acer palmatum *"Dissectum," is the perfect choice for this container.*

Tools

A small **gardener's trowel** is all that you need to dig holes ready for planting.

A **watering can** with a long neck is preferable. The longer the spout the better, since the flow of water is easier to control. A nozzle with fine holes is essential to give the plants a good drenching without damage. There is a wide range of watering cans available, from bright red plastic ones to green metal ones.

A **hose**, with a spray attachment, is useful when a large number of containers are involved. Some very good fine spray attachments are now available.

A **sealant gun** is essential for applying the waterproof sealant to cracks and holes in containers when creating a water garden (see the project on page 36).

Feeding

With a good potting soil, there is no need to add fertilizer at planting time, but because watering washes many of the nutrients out of the soil, feeding as growth progresses is essential.

A **general liquid fertilizer** throughout the summer, every other day, will keep a display going and help winter- and spring-flowering plants to build up their strength. However, any arrangement that is to continue through the winter should not be fed in late summer and fall, since this encourages soft sappy growth, easily cut back by frost.

Controlled-release fertilizers in the form of tablets and capsules, which are pressed down into the soil at planting time, are effective over a long period, slowly releasing their nutrients into the compost.

Materials

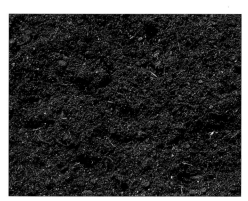

Peat-based potting soil

Peat-based potting soil has always been the first choice for most containers. It has the advantage of being light and, therefore, ideal in hanging baskets, containers which are intended to be moved around, and in roof gardens or balconies. The disadvantage is that it dries out very quickly so plants growing in it must be watered frequently. However, peat is extracted from peat beds, and there has been much environmental damage. Some peat beds are now being managed, so the best approach would be to seek out a manufacturer with a sound environmental policy. There are also some alternative soils now appearing, based around shredded forest bark, and these would be an excellent choice.

Crockery shards are needed for drainage in the bottom of containers. The best are broken pieces of terracotta flowerpots, although broken tiles or medium-size stones collected from the garden would also suffice.

Moss is used to line hanging baskets. It is easily obtainable from garden centers; an alternative source is to use moss raked from the lawn, but you must make sure that no chemicals have been used to treat the grass.

Broken flowerpots make the best shards.

Coir, or coconut fiber, is sold as a viable alternative to peat; however, there is now a question mark over this because the soil in its native environment is being impoverished by its removal.

Moss

Soil-based potting soil, being very heavy, should only be used in containers which are permanently sited and not on roof gardens or balconies. It has the advantage of drying out more slowly.

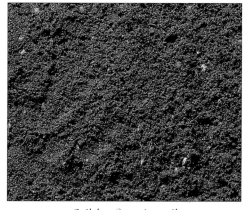

Soil-based potting soil

Watering

A regular water regime is most important. The main reason for container plants failing is that they have not been watered sufficiently. In hot weather, they need watering twice a day: once in the morning and again in the evening. Continue watering until a puddle appears under the container, which may take a minute or two, depending on the size of the container.

Wind can have a serious drying effect, particularly on hanging baskets. In hot or warm windy weather, these containers will need watering three times daily: morning, early afternoon,

It is much easier to control the flow of water with a long spout on the watering can.

and evening. In severe weather, it would be best to remove the basket to a sheltered spot, returning it later when the weather becomes more clement.

In **normal weather** conditions, check the top of the soil with your finger, and only water the plant if it is not damp to the touch.

Care should be taken to avoid splashing water on the leaves because this can cause them to scorch in the sun.

Soil additives, which hold water and release it slowly to the plants, are useful if you are unable to water your plants for a day or two.

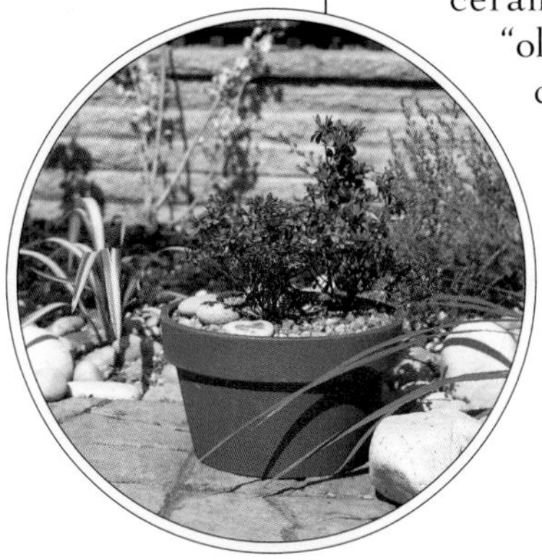

Where the local soil conditions are unfavorable to them, some plants are better grown in containers. This acid-loving azalea is much happier in a container with acid soil than in the local chalky soil.

Garden Design

RICHARD KEY

Containers can add height and impact to a small sitting area.

Containers are useful tools for the designer, and growing plants in ornamental containers allows flexibility in layout and a variety of heights anywhere in the garden, as well as adding color and interest all year round.

Interest can be added to any garden, large or small, and planted containers are a quick way of "furnishing" the patio. They may be used in various ways, perhaps singly to enhance a specimen plant or as an eye-catching focal point; in pairs either side of a door or archway, or framing a view or flight of steps; sited in groups to create bold effects, or to link the house with the terrace and garden; or on the walls around the edge of a patio to create a bright view which is easy to maintain.

Containers need not be planted to be effective. This terra-cotta urn has been discreetly, but effectively, used in a border situation.

The **color** of container plants can transform the bleakest concrete corner into a green and refreshing oasis. On patios, steps, roof terraces, and even tiny balconies, the colors, scents, textures, and sometimes tastes provided by planted containers offer a soft, friendly, inviting environment. It only takes a little know-how and imagination to turn a large ceramic bowl, wooden trough, or "old" chimney pot into a blaze of color, which can be used as an attractive feature in a small garden or to cheer up a patio or balcony.

Some plants have a very spectacular, but short, flowering season and are very untidy for the rest of the year. Plants like lilies, herbs, and vegetables are best displayed when they are at their best, and then the bulbs kept until the next season. Other plants, like agapanthus, flower better in containers and should also only appear in high summer. Tender plants, like fuchsias and geraniums, will need frost protection in the winter, and in containers they can easily be moved to a warmer spot. This mobile form of gardening is an essential part of the gardener's repertoire. Acid-loving plants, like azaleas and rhododendrons, can be grown in containers, using ericaceous compost, where the prevailing soil is alkaline.

Hanging baskets and **wall baskets** are always eye-catching and provide a quick way of brightening up a wall or trellis, without taking up too much space. Planted with herbs or vegetables, and sited close to the kitchen door, they will serve a useful purpose, as well as an ornamental one.

An **all-year garden** can be created by planting evergreens in containers. Attractive arrangements can be created by combining shrubs, dwarf conifers, and perennials, with larger specimens planted in larger tubs, permanently placed. Interesting effects can be created by underplanting with a succession of bulbs, and bedding plants in summer, for color throughout the year.

Single containers can be placed with other plants to add color and interest.

SUMMER CASCADE

This spectacular way of growing plants, discovered in an old gardening book, is also an excellent way of growing herbs and alpines. Since it is to be viewed from one side only, a

cascade on either side of a doorway is a perfect way of enhancing bare walls, and one can be used very effectively as a centerpiece for a group of containers against a wall on a patio.

Materials

Five terra-cotta pots, one each of diameter 16½ inches; 14 inches; 10 inches; 7 inches; 5 inches • Crockery shards • Peat-based or lightweight potting soil (so container is light to move)

QUICK TIPS

Planting time: spring **Light:** sun

Care: it is important to keep the compost moist, so plants can draw water and nutrients from the reservoir of compost under each pot.

This scheme is made up of annuals and tender perennials, and will need replanting each spring. Bring the fuchsia and geraniums into a frost-free environment during the winter, since these plants are half-hardy.

Life expectancy: one summer season, but several years for the fuchsia and geraniums if protected from frost.

The Plants

The flowers of the fuchsia contrast delightfully with the pale or dark blue trailing lobelia and white sweet alyssum. The trailing pink-flowered geraniums trail down the sides of the pot to mingle with the trailing pink trumpet-shaped flowers of the petunias.

GRAHAM A. PAVEY

5 surfinia petunias (Petunia "Pink Mini"*)*

GRAHAM A. PAVEY

1 Fuchsia "Winston Churchill"

AN ALTERNATIVE PLANTING

For a warm sunny spot, to give a striking one-color display throughout the summer, plant rosemary (*Rosmarinus officinalis* "Miss Jessopp's Upright") to replace the fuchsia; 3 red busy lizzies to replace the trailing lobelia, and 3 to replace the sweet alyssum; 3 red ivy-leaf geraniums to replace the geraniums, and 4 to replace the petunias. When the season is over, plant the rosemary out in the open ground.

GRAHAM A. PAVEY

6 white sweet alyssum (Lobularia maritima, previously known as Alyssum maritimum)

GRAHAM A. PAVEY

5 trailing lobelia (Lobelia erinus pendula)

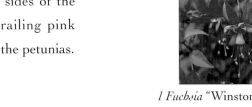

GRAHAM A. PAVEY

6 ivy-leaf geraniums (Pelargonium "Little Gem"*)*

1. Collect together the five differently sized containers. The traditional flowerpot shape is best because the rim adds stability to the arrangement.

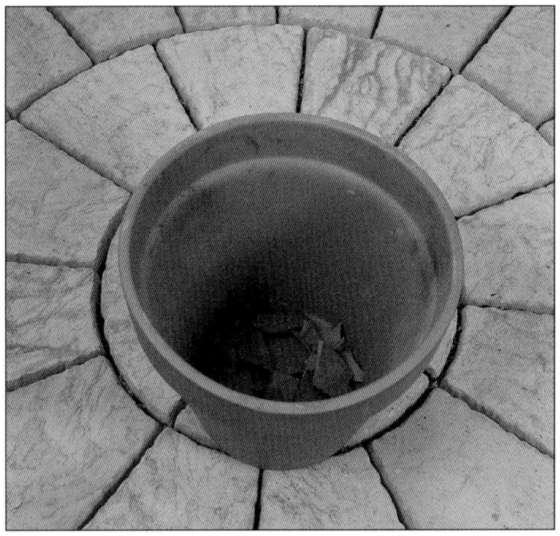

2. Starting with the largest pot, cover the base of the pot with a generous layer of crockery shards to aid drainage.

3. Add sufficient compost to allow the next largest pot to sit inside the first comfortably. Make sure the compost is well consolidated for stability.

4. Holding the second container in place, add compost to the first in the space created between the two. Again make sure that the compost is pressed down firmly to hold the second pot in place. Continue in this way until all the pots are filled.

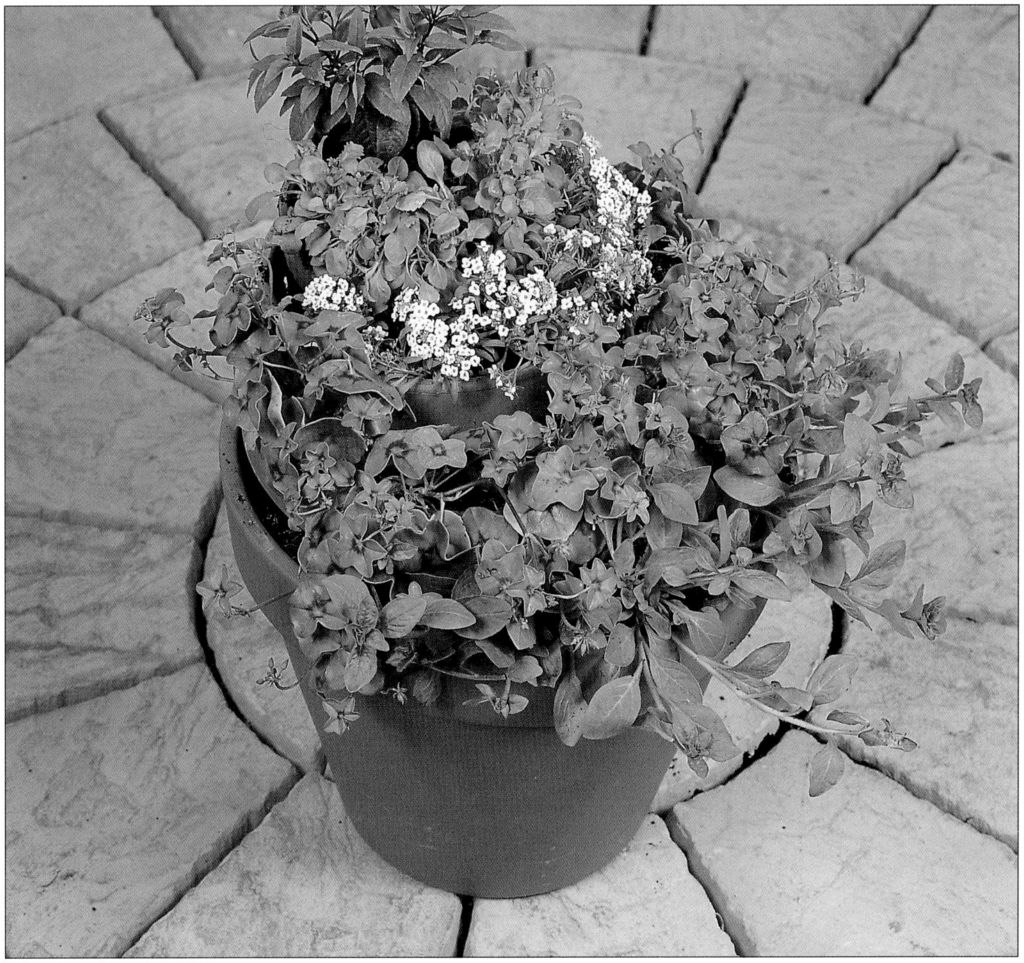

5. Starting at the top, plant the upright fuchsia in the smallest pot and the 5 trailing lobelia in the second layer. The 6 sweet alyssum in the third layer will grow through the trailing lobelia.

6. The 6 ivy-leaf geraniums in the fourth layer will grow through the lobelia and trail down the side of the container, where it will combine with the petunias. After planting, water thoroughly to help firm in the plants and remove any air pockets.

EVERGREEN FLOWERPOT

By using evergreens, we can insure color in the container throughout the year. Here, we have used larger garden plants which will give a colorful display for many years before

outgrowing the container and needing to be planted in the open ground. The pot should be brought in close to the house, or a path, where it can be enjoyed all the year round.

Materials

A terra-cotta pot, diameter 16½ inches • Crockery shards • Peat- or soil-based potting soil

QUICK TIPS

Planting time: spring or fall
Light: sun or shade

Care: if placed in a sunny position, the container will require watering at least once a day. In winter, it will require watering once a month and would benefit from some protection from frost in colder areas.
Life expectancy: the plants can stay in the pot for at least 3 years with an annual top dressing of compost. Eventually, when the plants become too large for the pot, they should be planted out into the garden.

The Plants

The *choisya,* with its scented white flowers in late spring and early summer followed by occasional blooms throughout the summer, has finely divided leaves, which are a good foil for many perennials and shrubs. Underneath, the variegated ivies and the periwinkles cascade down the sides of the container, the white variegation contrasting with the terra-cotta of the container and the azure blue flowers of the vinca in spring.

1 Choisya "Aztec Pearl"

3 periwinkles
(Vinca minor "Azurea Flore Pleno"*)*

3 variegated ivies
(Hedera helix "Glacier"*)*

1. Cover the base of the container with crockery shards to aid with drainage.

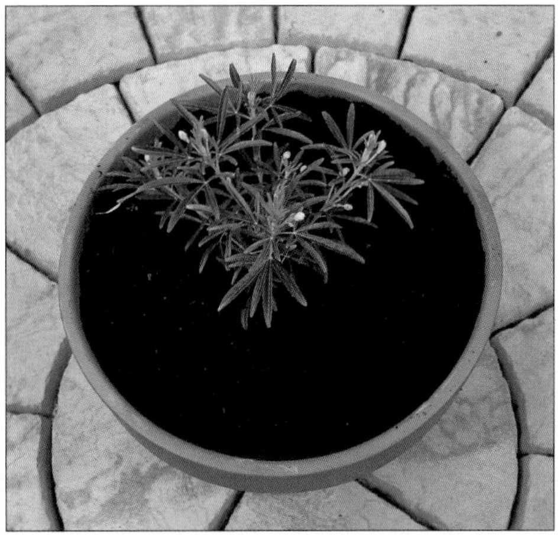

2. Fill the container to approximately 2½ inches below the rim to aid watering, making sure the compost is well consolidated. Plant the choisya in the center of the container.

3. Plant the 3 periwinkles, equally spaced around the outside of the container.

4. Finish the container with 3 ivies planted in the gaps between the vinca.

AN ALTERNATIVE PLANTING

This container has the added advantage of containing shade-loving plants. Plant 1 *Elaeagnus pungens* "Maculata" in place of the choisya, 3 *Liriope muscari* in place of the periwinkles, and 3 *Pachysandra terminalis* "Variegata" to replace the variegated ivies.

5. After planting, water thoroughly to firm up the soil. The finished container will quickly fill out, and will provide color from the moment it is planted up.

WINTER WINDOW BOX

A window box is perfect for brightening up any house. Try siting one at each window and planting each with an identical planting scheme. When the winter

pansies have finished, you could plant the box with trailing red ivy-leaf geraniums in the spring, to create a stunning effect in midsummer.

Materials

A window box about 30 inches x 6½ inches high x 8 inches deep • Crockery shards • Peat-based potting soil

QUICK TIPS

Planting time: spring
Light: sun or partial shade

Care: an occasional watering is all that will be necessary. Deadheading helps to keep a continuity of blooms.
Life expectancy: one winter season.

The Plants

Yellow winter-flowering pansies add a bright and cheerful splash of color all winter long.

GRAHAM A. PAVEY

12 yellow winter flowering pansies (Viola tricolor)

1. First, if the bottom of the box has no drainage holes, drill one at each end, 2 inches in diameter. Cover the bottom of the box with a layer of shards and fill with peat-based potting soil to approximately 2½ inches from the top.

2. Plant the pansies close together until the whole box is filled. You will need 12 plants for a box this size.

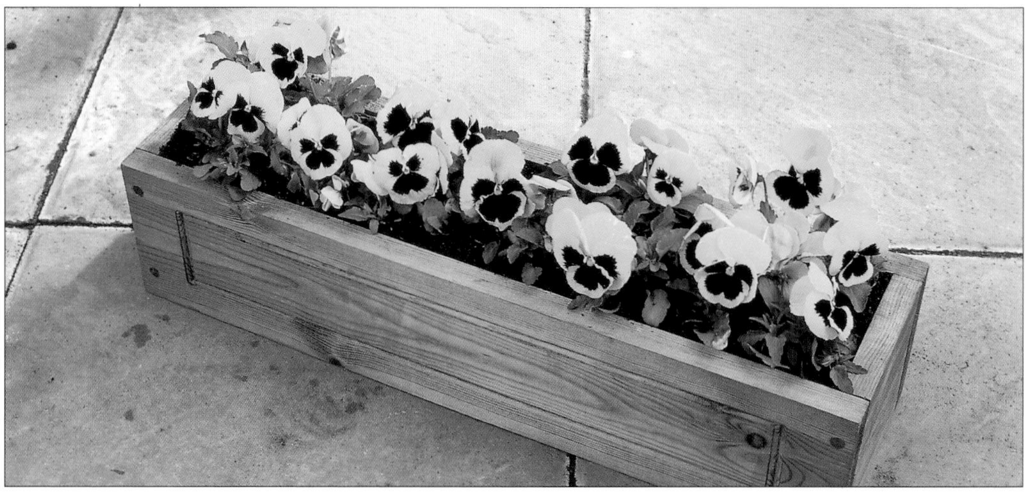

3. After planting, water thoroughly.

4. Winter-flowering pansies will flower all winter, flowering even better after a very cold spell.

Springtime Half-pot

Although mainly spring-flowering, this container has evergreen interest all the year round. It flowers from mid-fall to early summer, and should be placed where it can be seen during that period, near a frequently used path or doorway.

Materials

1 terra-cotta half-pot 14½ inches x 9 inches • Crockery shards • Peat-based potting soil

QUICK TIPS

Planting time: fall, or when potted daffodils are obtainable
Light: sun or shade

Care: after the daffodils have finished flowering, the leaves help to build up the store of food in the bulb for flowering the following year, so this is a good time to liquid feed. The leaves should be allowed to die down naturally. When they have turned brown, remove them from the plant.

Throughout the summer months, water daily in hot weather and feed once a week with liquid fertilizer. Do not neglect it during its dormant season.

Life expectancy: the laurustinus is a large garden plant and will outgrow the container in a couple of years, when it should be planted out into the garden. At this point, replant the arrangement.

The Plants

The laurustinus, one of the longest flowering shrubs, flowers from fall through to mid-spring when the daffodils are then at their best, and the evergreen white rock cress is starting to flower from late spring to early summer.

AN ALTERNATIVE PLANTING

Plant a *Prunus lusitanica* "Variegata" in the center of the container, surrounded by 8 *Narcissus* "Thalia" and 12 *Aubretia deltoidea*.

1 laurustinus (Viburnum tinus)

8 daffodils (Narcissus "Jack Snipe"*)*
A small yellow daffodil

12 rock cress (Arabis caucasica)
A gray-leaved low-growing rock plant with white flowers in early summer

1. Place shards in the bottom of the container and add potting soil. Plant the laurustinus in the center, with the top of the rootball about 2½ inches lower than the top of the pot.

2. Add soil to just below the top of the laurustinus rootball. Plant the 8 daffodil bulbs, equally spaced around the edge of the rootball, with the base of each bulb being about 6 inches below the top of the soil. Take care to insure each bulb is the right way up.

3. Bring the potting soil up to the top of the rootball, firming gently, and plant the 12 rock cress around the perimeter, to cascade down the side of the container.

4. After planting, give the container a good watering to help firm in the plants. The arrangement will start to make a contribution quite quickly, and can be placed in its position immediately.

5. In spring, the daffodils will be at their best, the laurustinus will still be flowering, and the rock cress will be starting to flower. The leaves of the daffodils should be allowed to die down naturally.

6. In summer, the daffodils will have died down, but the rock cress will take over until later in the season, while the laurustinus will provide height and stability.

Summertime Stone Trough

Classical stone troughs of this size and shape can be difficult to plant up successfully. The final result of this project is subtle, but very effective, and especially so, sited on top of a low wall with a collection of containers grouped around the base of the wall.

Materials

A stone trough, about 32½ inches x 10½ inches high x 11½ inches deep • Crockery shards • Soil-based potting soil

QUICK TIPS

Planting time: spring
Light: sun or partial shade

Care: in hot weather, two waterings a day will be necessary; otherwise, one watering, first thing in the morning, should be sufficient. Feed with a liquid fertilizer every week.

The plants will need replanting on an annual basis. For winter color, remove these plants in the fall and replace with winter-flowering pansies.

Life expectancy: one summer season.

AN ALTERNATIVE PLANTING

Plant 12 blue lobelia (*Lobelia erinus*) to replace the sweet alyssum; 12 phlox (*Phlox drummondii*) to replace the verbenas;
9 tobacco plants (*Nicotiana* "Dwarf White Bedder") to replace the petunias; and 9 begonias (*Begonia semperflorens*) to replace the busy lizzies.

1. Plant up the container in its flowering position since it is very heavy and difficult to move.

Cover the bottom of the container with a layer of shards, and cover this with a layer of potting soil to approximately 2½ inches from the top. The extra weight of a soil-based potting soil will have little effect on an already-heavy container.

The Plants

White-centered red and pink flower clusters of verbenas, pink and mauve trumpets of petunias, and white sweet alyssum mingle with bright busy lizzies to provide a brilliant splash of color as summer unfolds, until the first frosts.

12 sweet alyssum (Lobularia maritima, previously known as Alyssum maritima)

GRAHAM A. PAVEY

12 verbenas (Verbena hybrida "Showtime"*)*

GRAHAM A. PAVEY

9 petunias (Petunia hybrida)

9 busy lizzies (Impatiens "Elfin Mix"*)*

2. Start by planting the busy lizzies, equally spaced around the container.

3. Tap each plant out of its container, and tease out the roots before planting to encourage quick new growth.

4. Fill in around the busy lizzies with the remaining plants, keeping the sweet alyssum close to the edge.

5. Water thoroughly after planting to remove any air pockets.

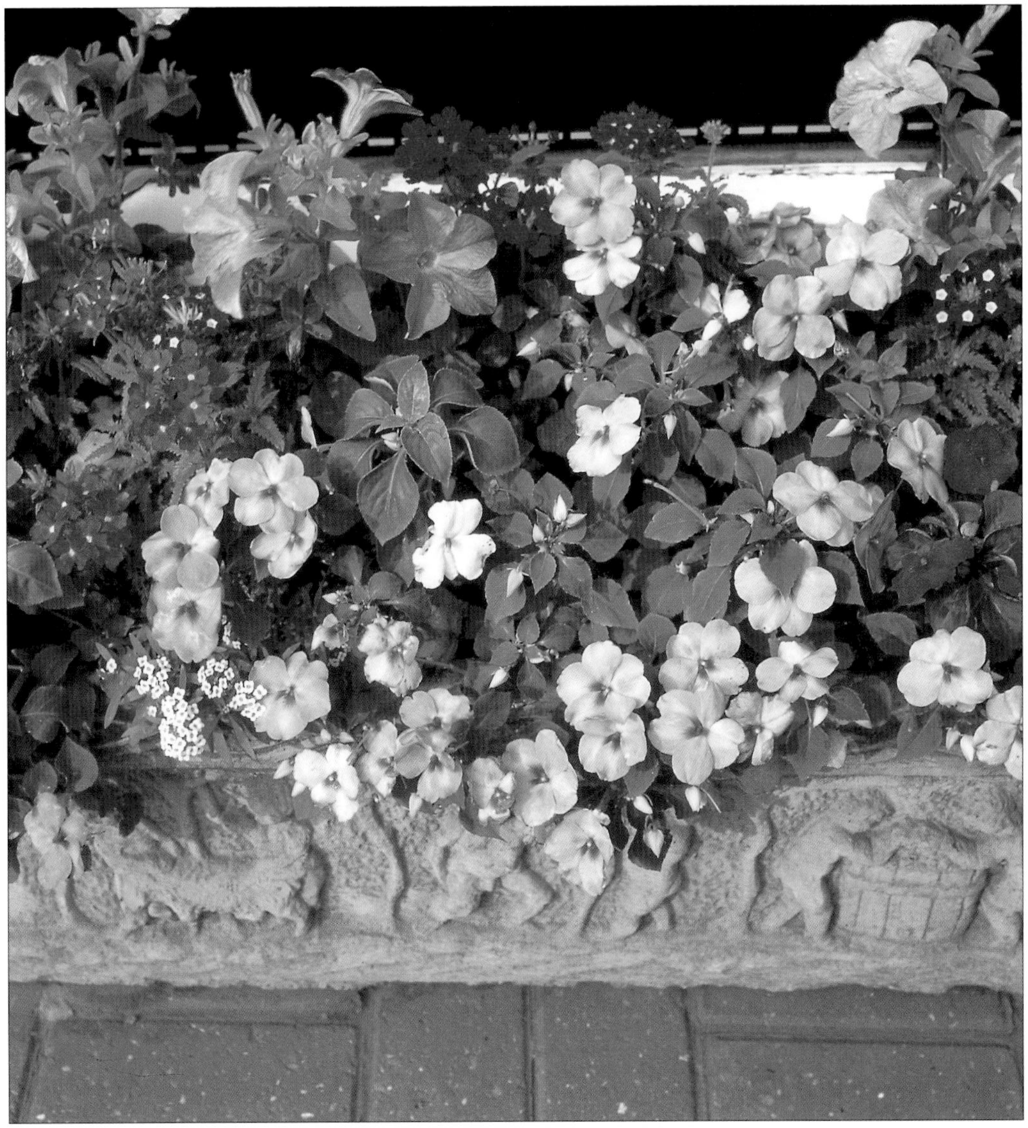

GARDEN MATTERS

6. The plants will grow away quickly, and the container will begin to contribute to the garden immediately.

SHADY CORNER HALF-POT

Although flowering in the winter, this arrangement has all-year-round interest and is perfect in a shady corner. Sweet box has a delightful vanilla scent which fills the air in

midwinter, lifting the spirit. It needs careful placing to be enjoyed to the full, ideally near a north-facing doorway with a little shelter from the wind to allow the scent to fill the air.

QUICK TIPS

Planting time: fall
Light: shade or partial shade

Care: tidy the arrangement in the spring, removing any dead leaves. Water sparingly throughout the winter, but regularly in the summer when the soil should be kept moist. Feed with a liquid fertilizer every week from spring to midsummer, but not later because it will encourage soft sappy growth.
Life expectancy: about three years.

Materials

1 terra-cotta half-pot about 14½ inches x 9 inches • Crockery shards • Peat-based potting soil

AN ALTERNATIVE PLANTING

This gold and purple arrangement needs similar conditions to the main plan, and will also be at its best in the winter. Plant 1 Mexican orange blossom (*Choisya ternata* "Sundance") to replace the sweet box; 3 bergenias (*Bergenia* "Ballawley Hybrid"); 3 lilyturf (*Liriope muscari*) to replace the ferns; and 3 golden creeping jennie (*Lysimachia nummularia* "Aureum") to replace the ivies.

1 sweet box
(Sarcococca humilis)

GARDEN MATTERS

3 heartleaf bergenias
(Bergenia cordifolia)

The Plants

Delightfully scented sweet box is surrounded by heartleaf bergenias, with their large, round, leathery leaves and pink flowers in spring. Soft-shield ferns, with their tall, feathery evergreen fronds, and variegated ivies add a light touch.

GARDEN MATTERS

3 soft-shield ferns
(Polystichum setiferum)

3 variegated ivies
(Hedera helix "Glacier"*)*

1. Line the base of the container with shards and fill with soil to within 2½ inches of the rim. Plant the main plant, a sweet box, in the center.

2. Plant 3 soft-shield ferns equally spaced around the edge. The divided leaves of this plant will add a soft touch to the arrangement.

3. Plant the heartleaf begonias equally spaced between the ferns. The round leaves contrast well with the other elements in the pot.

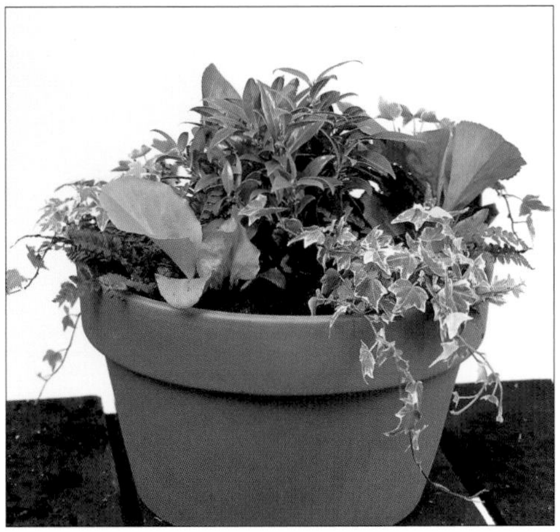

4. Finish off with the three ivies planted to cascade down the side of the container, their white variegation contrasting well with the red terracotta.

5. After planting, water thoroughly to consolidate the arrangement and remove any air pockets. The scheme will develop quite quickly and can be used immediately.

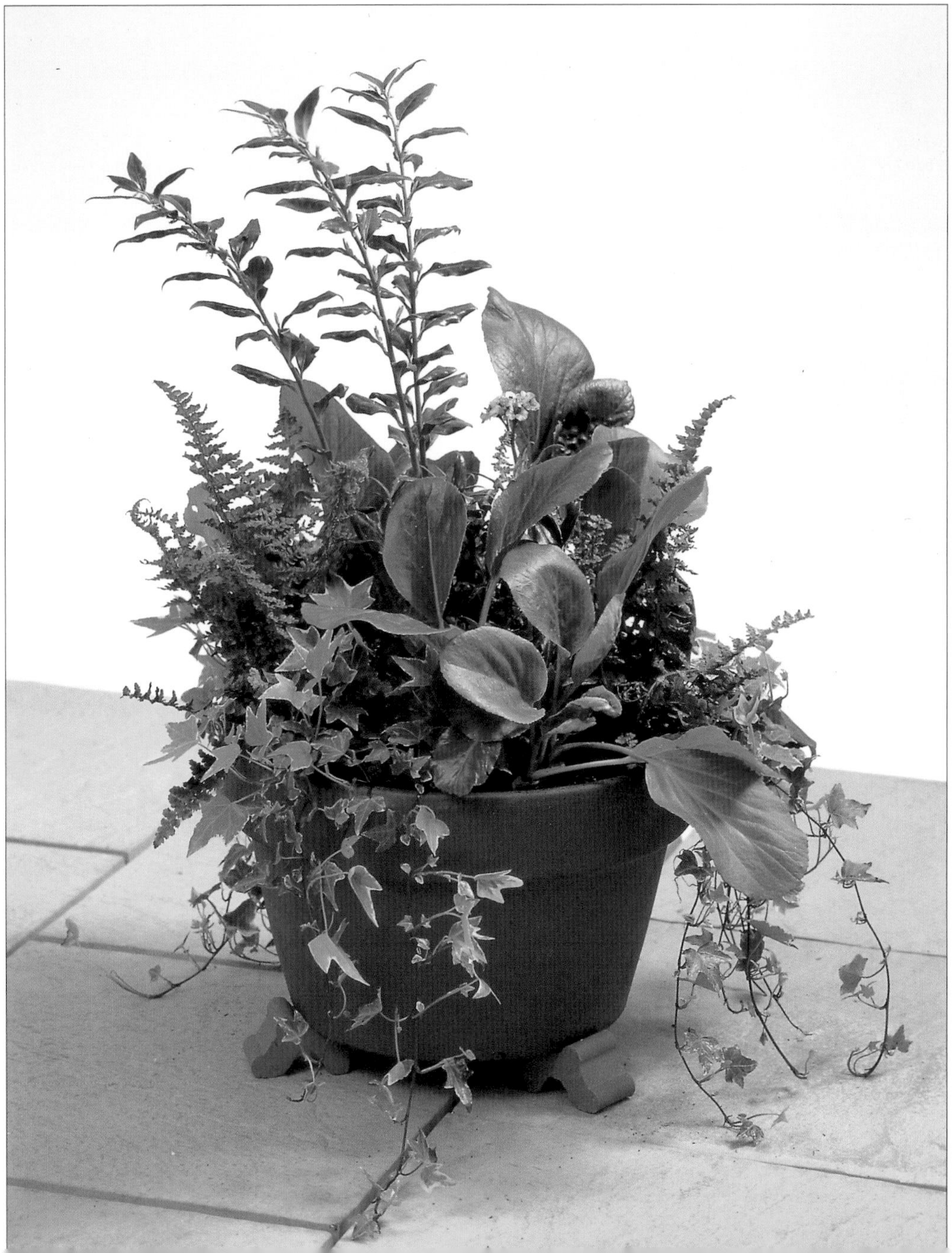

WINTER PYRAMID

A slow-growing conifer is an ideal subject for use in a container, not outgrowing it for several years. This arrangement is perhaps best placed

as a single container for a focal point, or on the corner of a path or beside a doorway. In the summer months, purple petunias could replace the pansies.

Materials

1 terra-cotta cylinder pot 15 inches diameter x 11 inches high • Crockery shards • Peat-based potting soil

1. Line the base of the container with crockery shards. Add soil to a level where the conifer sits comfortably, the top of its rootball 2½ inches lower than the rim. Remove the plant from its container by inverting it, squeezing the sides, and gently encouraging it out. Tease out the roots, and plant in the center of the arrangement.

QUICK TIPS

Planting time: fall
Light: better in full sun, but will grow in shade

Care: apart from replanting the pansies each year, the arrangement will need little attention. Conifers are thirsty, however, and need regular watering throughout the summer – two or three times a day if in an exposed position. Feed with a liquid fertilizer each week from spring through to midsummer.
Life expectancy: the conifer can remain in the container for up to five years or more, if the top layer of soil is replaced each spring. Replant the pansies each year, and the ivies every two or three years.

The Plants

Usually grown as single specimens, because they die back where other plants grow against them, conifers appear very formal. The answer is to grow annuals and bedding plants at their base, which are removed before any permanent damage can be done. Here, distinctive, large, round-faced purple winter pansies contrast well with ivy and the golden conifer foliage.

1 Thuja occidentalis "Sunkist"

GRAHAM A. PAVEY

6 purple winter pansies (Viola tricolor)

3 variegated ivies (Hedera helix "Glacier"*)*

2. Plant the ivies equally spaced around the edge to grow down the side of the container.

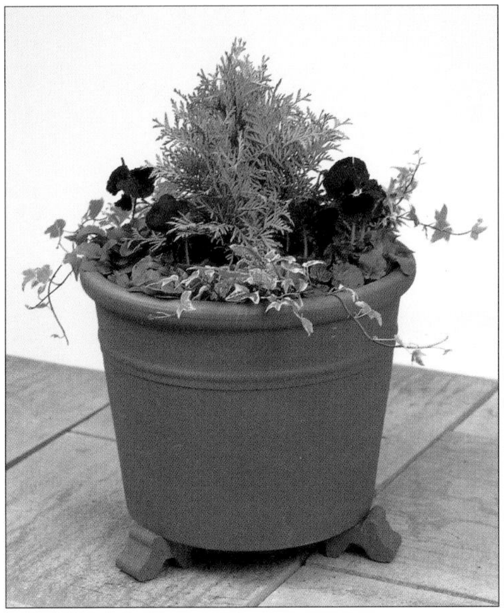

3. Infill with the pansies. After planting, water thoroughly to consolidate the roots, before placing it in position in the garden.

4. As the scheme develops, it will form a pyramid shape with the ivies eventually hiding the container.

SUMMER HANGING BASKET

Hanging baskets have become very popular, with an industry growing up around them. Nurseries compete to produce new and unusual plants to grow in them, and manufacturers find new ways of watering them. This hanging basket is very traditional and a proven favorite, offering a high degree of success. Almost as successful are begonias (Begonia semperflorens) planted instead of busy lizzies. Hanging baskets can be very effective if suspended from the crosspieces along the side of a pergola.

1. Press moss into the base of the basket, bringing it up the sides to the level where the first layer of plants will be added.

2. Plant 4 busy lizzies, equally spaced around the basket. Squeeze the root-balls, as necessary, to push them between the wires.

Materials

A hanging basket, 14 inches in diameter • Moss • A sheet of plastic • Peat-based potting soil

QUICK TIPS

Planting time: spring
Light: sun or shade

Care: it is difficult to overwater busy lizzies, but they soon complain if underwatered, drooping quite markedly. Under normal conditions, water twice daily and three or four times in very hot conditions. Feed with a liquid fertilizer every other day.
Life expectancy: one summer season. Busy lizzies are tender perennials and could be grown on through the winter in frost-free conditions, but the plants are usually past their prime by the fall and best discarded.

The Plants

Busy lizzies are also happy growing in shade, although the arrangement will become more open as they grow.

12 busy lizzies
(Impatiens "Elfin Mix"*)*

3. Cut out a circle from the plastic (the soil bag would be a perfect source). Make three holes in it to insure the potting soil is kept moist, but not waterlogged, and place it on the bed of moss in the bottom of the basket.

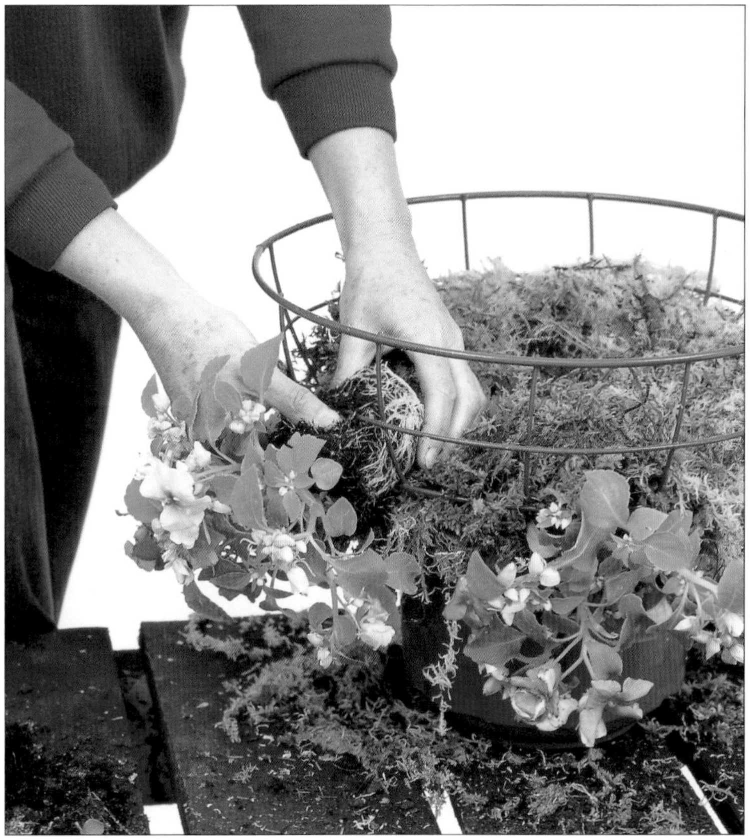

4. Build the moss up the side of the container to the next level of planting, and plant 4 more busy lizzies between those already planted.

5. Add more moss, bringing it up to 2½ inches above the top of the basket to create a "dish" in the center, and thereby aid watering. Fill the center with potting soil, firming and consolidating the plants and moss around the perimeter.

6. Finish the container by planting 4 busy lizzies in the top, and water well to consolidate the plants.

7. The finished container can be used immediately, although it should not be exposed to frost and may be better grown on in a greenhouse until all danger has passed.

8. As the season unfolds, the basket will fill out to form a complete ball of color.

SUMMER WALL BASKET

Old hay racks, originally used for feeding livestock, make ideal planting containers, but newly manufactured versions are, perhaps, the easiest to obtain.

A single basket can look a little lost, so it is a good idea to use several, equally spaced on a long wall, with a similar planting in each.

An ideal place to grow herbs, a basket of this nature could be installed in the kitchen, handy to the cook, placed close to a window to give it plenty of light.

Materials

A wall basket, 16 inches in diameter • Moss • A sheet of plastic • Peat-based potting soil

QUICK TIPS

Planting time: spring **Light:** full sun

Care: as with all baskets, drying out is its biggest enemy. Keep well watered, especially in hot and windy conditions when three waterings a day will be required. Under normal conditions, water in the morning and again in the evening, and feed with a liquid fertilizer every other day.
Life expectancy: one summer season.

AN ALTERNATIVE PLANTING

Plant a trailing fuchsia to replace the ivy-leaf geranium; and a zonal geranium to replace the upright fuchsia. Plant 4 white trailing lobelia to replace the blue trailing lobelia; 3 white sweet alyssum to replace the busy lizzies; 3 lobelia to replace the verbenas; and a creeping jennie (*Lysimachia nummularia*) to replace the catnip.

The Plants

Pink, red, and white verbenas, busy lizzies, and an upright fuchsia combine with trailing catnip, blue lobelia, and a pink ivy-leaf geranium.

GRAHAM A. PAVEY

3 verbenas (Verbena hybrida "Showtime"*)*

GRAHAM A. PAVEY

3 busy lizzies (Impatiens "Elfin Mix"*)*

GRAHAM A. PAVEY

1 upright fuchsia. Fuchsias have bell-shaped flowers of red, pink, purple, and white all summer

GRAHAM A. PAVEY

4 trailing lobelia (Lobelia erinus pendula) A trailing plant with pale or dark blue flowers

1 ivy-leaf geranium (Pelargonium peltatum "Abel Carriere"*)*

1 trailing catnip (Nepeta hederacea)

1. Place a layer of moss across the bottom of the container to make sure the contents do not fall out between the bars, and to hold moisture like a sponge. Cut a circle of plastic from the sheet or soil bag, make three holes in it, and place it on top of the moss. The plastic will help to maintain the moisture level, and the holes will insure that the compost does not become waterlogged.

2. Bring the moss up to the desired level for planting the "side" plants in a thin layer of soil – about halfway up the container. Carefully insert the rootball of the ivy-leaf geranium through the bars – if necessary, squash the rootball to gain access. Plant the 4 trailing lobelia in the same way.

3. Continue to add moss, carefully consolidating it around the roots of the plants already planted. Finish the moss off at about 2½ inches above the rim of the basket to create a hollow to aid watering.

4. Add a layer of compost, and plant the fuchsia in the center of the basket.

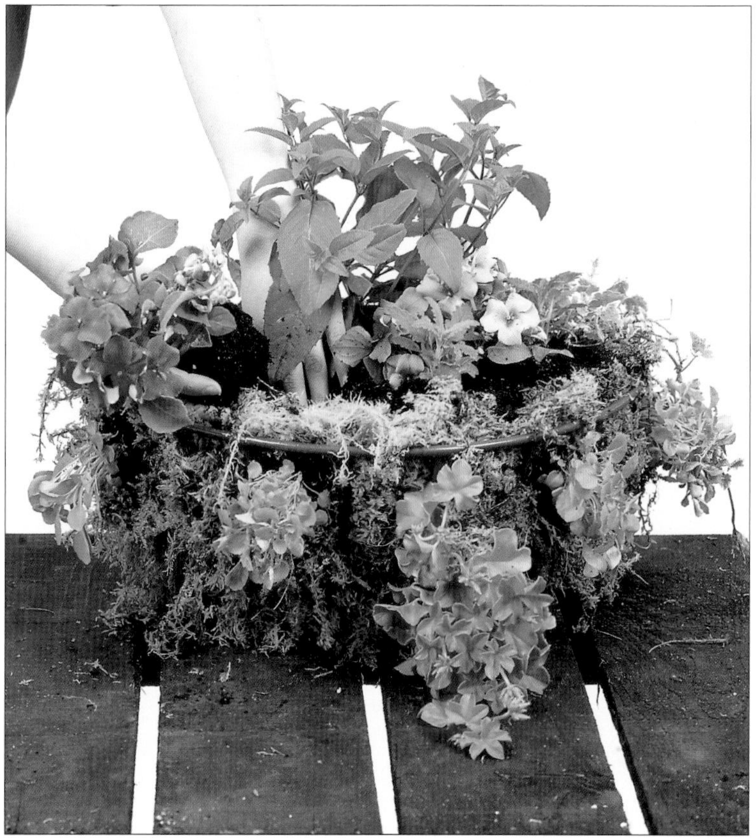

5. Plant the 3 busy lizzies and 3 verbenas around the fuchsia, and a single trailing catnip plant on one side. This vigorous plant will trail down to the ground and looks better planted alone on one side of the container.

6. The final container will require two screws or nails attached to a wall or fence for hanging. When planted, the container will make a contribution to the garden immediately.

7. Water well after planting to consolidate the arrangement. As the container develops, it will fill out, forming a large ball which, with careful attention, will flower throughout the summer.

WINTER HANGING BASKET

When the summer basket has finished, there is no need to store it away until the following spring – why not plant it up for the winter? This arrangement uses evergreens and could be maintained throughout the year, although it may appear a little dull in the summer. Hang it close to a frequently used north-facing door or path, where its scent and sight can be enjoyed all winter.

Materials

A hanging basket, 14 inches in diameter • Moss • A sheet of plastic • Peat-based potting soil

QUICK TIPS

Planting time: fall
Light: partial shade

Care: water sparingly throughout the winter, when the compost feels dry to the touch. Because of the checkerberries, only rainwater should be used.
Life expectancy: about two years. After this, move the plants to the open ground and replant the container.

AN ALTERNATIVE PLANTING

This scheme requires similar conditions, but it will not be necessary to water with rainwater. Plant 1 Alexandrian laurel (*Danae racemosa*) to replace the sweet box, and 2 carpet bugles (*Ajuga reptans* "Atropurpurea") to replace the thymes. Plant 2 saxifrages (*Saxifraga moschata* "Cloth of Gold") to replace the violas; 2 creeping jennies (*Lysimachia nummularia*) to replace the ivies; and 2 *Sisyrinchium bellum* to replace the checkerberries.

The Plants

The vanilla-scented flowers of the sweet box can be enjoyed in midwinter, while the acid-loving checkerberries will colonize the top of the soil and even hang over the edge. The red berries contrast with the flowers of the violas and the variegated colors of the ivy.

2 violas (Viola labradorica)

1 sweet box (Sarcococca humilis)

2 wooly thymes (Thymus pseudolanuginosus)

2 checkerberries (Gaultheria procumbens)

2 variegated ivies (Hedera helix "Glacier"*)*

1. Build up the container using the same method as for the summer basket (see page 26). Plant the 2 wooly thymes and 2 violas alternately in the side of the basket.

2. Plant the sweet box in the center. Plant the variegated ivies to hang over the edge.

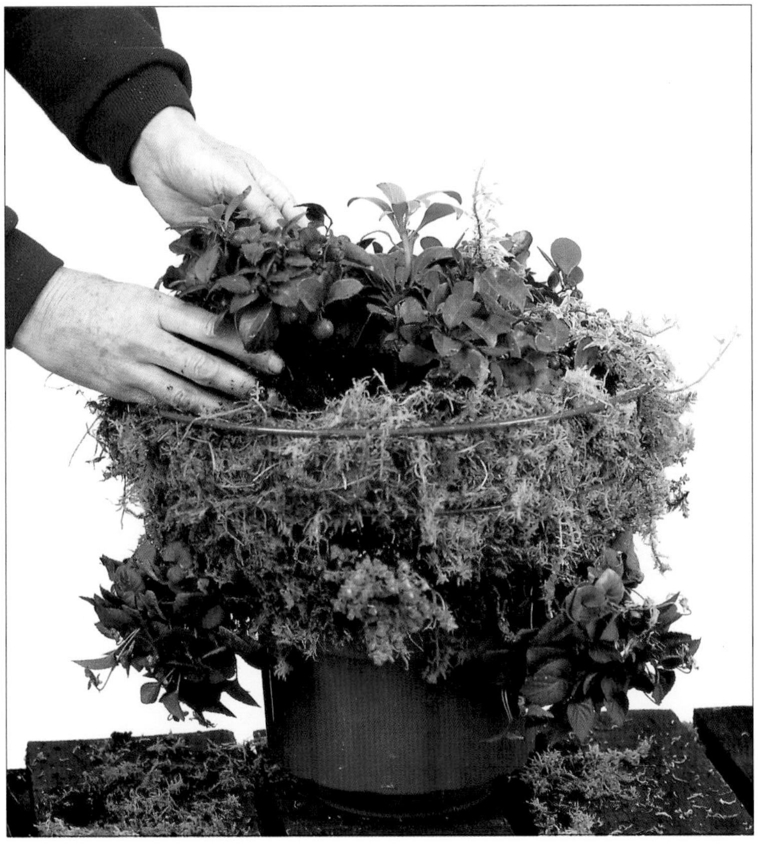

3. Finish the arrangement with the 2 checkerberries planted in between the ivies.

4. Water thoroughly with rainwater to remove any air pockets. The basket will take a few weeks to fill out, and may need some encouragement in a cool greenhouse.

HERB FLOWERPOT

Herbs in containers can be placed close to where they are needed, and this arrangement has been designed to be ornamental as well as functional, offering all-year-round interest. This container is the perfect choice as the central feature in a group of three: a rosemary in a medium-size container and a sage in a smaller one placed in front of it. The whole group looks good in the corner of a warm sunny patio.

Materials

A terra-cotta flowerpot, 16½ inches in diameter

• Crockery shards • Peat-based potting soil

QUICK TIPS

Planting time: spring, ideally, or as required
Light: sun or partial shade

Care: each morning check the soil for moisture with a fingertip, and only water if dry.
Life expectancy: the finished scheme can be left untouched for approximately two years before any serious maintenance will be required. At this time, it would be best to remove the lower planting, add some fresh soil, and replant.

AN ALTERNATIVE PLANTING

Plant a rosemary (*Rosmarinus officinalis* "Miss Jessopp's Upright") to replace the bay; 3 gold-splashed oregano (*Oreganum vulgare* "Gold Tip") to replace the thyme; 3 chives (*Allium schoenoprasum*) (there are no substitutes for chives); and 3 thymes (*Thymus serpyllum* "Annie Hall") to replace the creeping jennie.

The Plants

Herbs are perfect plants for container-growing. Many come from hot, dry countries, and the oil in their leaves, which gives their aroma and taste, evaporates more slowly than water, allowing them to cope with neglect better than other plants.

1 bay (Laurus nobilis)

GRAHAM A. PAVEY

3 creeping jennie (Lysimachia nummularia)

3 chives (Allium schoenoprasum)

3 lemon thyme (Thymus × citriodorus "Variegata")

1. Place a layer of crockery shards in the bottom of the container and add compost. Remove the main plant, a bay, from its pot by inverting it and gently squeezing, or tapping, until the rootball drops out. Tease out the roots to prepare it for planting. Add potting soil to a level where the plant sits comfortably, the top of its rootball 2½ inches lower than the rim of the container. Fill around the plant with potting soil, firming as you go, up to the top of the rootball.

2. Plant the 3 thymes evenly spaced around the edge. The variegated leaves of this plant will be enhanced by the backdrop of the bay leaves, and will stand out well against the terra-cotta.

3. Creeping jennie can become a nuisance when grown in the open ground. In a container, it can be allowed to grow down the side and is easily controlled by the occasional trim. Plant 3 around the edge, one next to each thyme.

4. Shape and texture are an important element of planting design, and containers are no exception to these rules. Chives are the only herb with an upright, spiky texture, and they will add impact to the arrangement.

5. Water the container well after planting, and allow a month before harvesting the herbs. It offers immediate interest, and the chive flowers begin to appear in late spring and early summer.

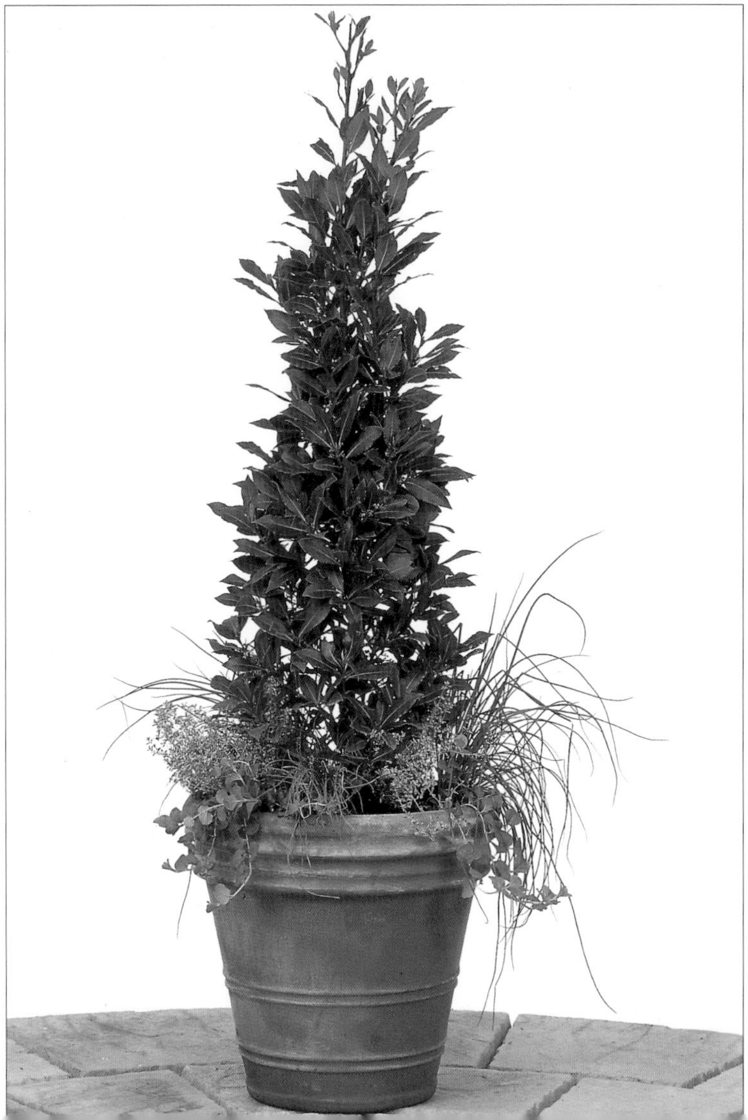

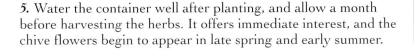

SUMMER WOODEN HALF-BARREL

Half-barrels can be difficult to plant up effectively, but this scheme makes an attractive summer planting simply by using two varieties of plants. One on either side of a warm, sunny doorway would be the perfect choice.

Because this is a scheme for summer, and the container may be difficult to move, it is a good idea to dig up and overwinter these tender perennials in a frost-free place. Replant the container for winter color when the summer display has finished.

Materials

A half-barrel, about 14 inches high x 20 inches diameter • Crockery shards • Peat- or soil-based potting soil

QUICK TIPS

Planting time: spring **Light:** full sun

Care: the arrangement will need watering twice a day in very hot weather, but in normal conditions, once first thing in the morning. Feed with a liquid fertilizer twice a week to keep the flowers coming.

These perennial plants can be grown through the winter in a frost-free sunroom or porch. Otherwise, reduce the watering to once a month and bring the container into a frost-free shed or outbuilding to overwinter. If the container is a permanent fixture, remove all the plants and overwinter them separately.

Life expectancy: if winter protection is provided and some of the compost is replaced each spring, this container will give enjoyment for several years.

The Plants

Small bell-shaped flowers adorn the abutilon, and the trailing ivy-leaf geraniums are soon covered with pink flowers to fill the container to overflowing all summer long.

1 abutilon
(Abutilon "Kentish Belle"*)*

GRAHAM A. PAVEY

8 pink ivy-leaf geraniums
(Pelargonium peltatum)

AN ALTERNATIVE PLANTING

This alternative planting, for winter color, uses a standard *Euonymus* "Silver Queen" to replace the abutilon, and 16 red winter pansies to replace the geraniums.

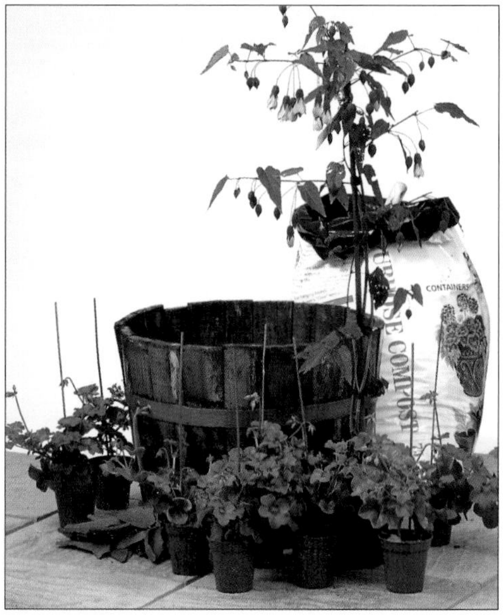

1. Spread a layer of crockery shards across the base of the half-barrel, and fill with potting soil. Use soil-based if the container is to remain where it is permanently, and peat-based if it is to be moved around. Remove the abutilon from its pot by inverting it and squeezing the sides. Gently tease out the roots before planting it toward the back of the container. Leave any supporting stake on to give the plant height.

2. Plant geraniums to fill up the rest of the container. Remove any supporting sticks to allow the plants to trail.

3. Water well after planting, and grow the container on in a frost-free place, moving it outside when all danger of frost has passed. If the container is permanently placed, do not plant up until the danger of frost has passed.

4. The container will flower the whole summer through, the geraniums quickly covering the wooden sides.

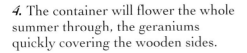

HYACINTH BOWL

Bowls of this nature look good when planted as small alpine gardens or with a single variety of bulb, such as bright red tulips (Tulipa praestans "Fusilier"). This project uses a single variety of hyacinths to create a spectacular effect in spring. It is effective on the corner of a patio or path, or in a group of three on a large patio. Three bowls of different sizes, each planted with a different single color, make a fine group.

Materials

A raised bowl, about 20 inches x 8 inches • Crockery shards • Peat-based potting soil

The Plants

These beautiful bright blue hyacinths will flower in early to mid-spring. A chemical in the bulb can irritate the skin, so use gloves when handling them, or protect your hand with a plastic bag.

GARDEN MATTERS

20 hyacinth bulbs (Hyacinthus orientalis "Amethyst"*)*

1. Place a layer of crockery shards in the bottom to cover the drainage hole.

2. Fill with potting soil to 4 inches below the top of the container. Press the 20 bulbs gently into the compost, evenly spaced around the bowl. Use a peat-based soil because this container will need moving out of sight when it has finished flowering.

QUICK TIPS

Planting time: fall
Light: shade or partial shade

Care: feed with a liquid fertilizer when the plants have finished flowering, and allow the leaves to die down naturally. Water occasionally throughout the summer.
Life expectancy: indefinite, as long as the maintenance regime is followed.

3. Finally, cover the bulbs and bring the level of compost up to 2½ inches below the rim of the bowl.

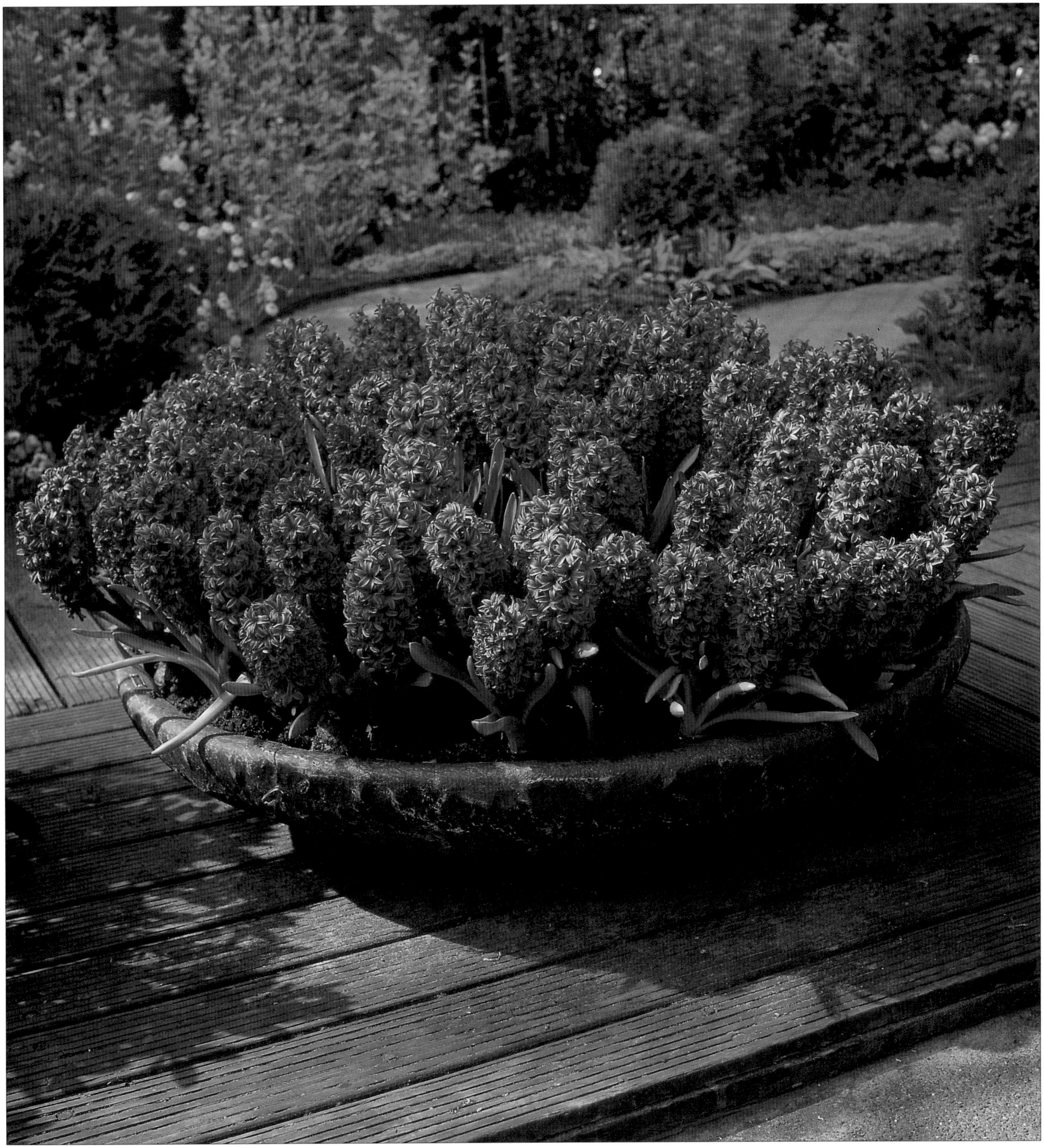

4. After planting, water thoroughly to settle the compost. Overwinter the bulbs in a cool greenhouse or shed.

WATER GARDEN

A container can be the perfect way to create a water garden where space is limited. It can look most effective as the central feature of an arrangement, surrounded with containers of plants,

such as grasses, bamboos, and hostas. The container could be sunk into the ground to create a water garden that is perfect for wildlife and makes an unusual addition to a flower border.

Materials

A container 15 inches high x 20 inches diameter • Waterproof sealant • Sealant gun • 3 engineering bricks • Gravel or small granite chips • 3 pieces of broken flowerpot or tile

QUICK TIPS

Planting time: spring
Light: sun or partial shade

Care: although the plants are hardy, it is best to give some winter protection, because expanding ice may damage the container.

The marginal plants (iris and marsh marigold) may need planting into larger plastic pots in time. Use a plastic basket available at a water-garden specialist and a proprietary water-garden soil or garden loam – ordinary potting soil will add too many nutrients to the water and encourage algae. There are chemicals available which keep the algae under control, and these should be added to the water, as long as livestock is not to be introduced.

Life expectancy: with the occasional tidy and repotting of the plants, this water feature should last for many years.

The Plants

It is important to select a dwarf water lily. A plant such as *Nymphaea alba* is a monster, only suitable for large ponds or lakes. Many water plants are quick colonizers, unsuitable for small containers, so careful selection is important.

GARDEN MATTERS

1 marsh marigold (Caltha palustris "Plena"*)*

GARDEN MATTERS

1 water lily (Nymphaea)

1 Japanese iris (Iris ensata "Variegata"*) (also known as Iris kaempferi* "Variegata"*)*

1. To make sure the container holds water, seal any holes and cracks with a waterproof sealant – the substance used for sealing around window frames. Apply a circle of sealant around each drainage hole, making sure that the contact area is clean beforehand.

2. Cover sealant with a piece of flowerpot or broken tile, pressed into place. Allow 24 hours for this to dry before adding water.

3. Add a layer of gravel. Use bricks as plinths for the plants to make sure they are sitting at the right height.

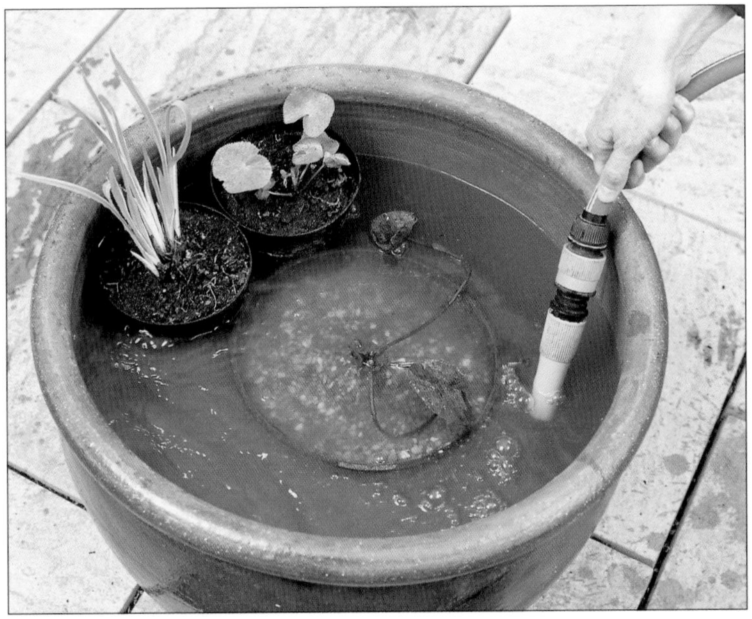

4. Place the plants, in their pots, on the bricks or gravel in the container. For the iris and marsh marigold, the top of the soil should be just below the surface of the water. The water lily should be deeper, sitting on the gravel, but it must be lowered in stages. Start it off at a level where the leaves float comfortably on the surface, then lower it slowly week by week as new growth appears. Adjust the plant height by adding or removing the gravel and bricks. Fill with water to the desired level. Keep the end of the hose under the water to reduce damaging turbulence.

AN ALTERNATIVE PLANTING

Half-barrels are perfect for this type of project. Seal the cracks between the slats with sealant to create a waterproof container. Plant this selection of less-invasive water plants: a sweet flag (*Acorus calamus* "Variegatus") to replace the iris; a water forget-me-not (*Myositis scorpioides*) to replace the marsh marigold; and a water lily (*Nymphaea* "Hermine").

5. If planted in the spring, a succession of color will start almost immediately with the yellow flowers of the marsh marigold and purple flowers of the iris, followed by water lilies in the summer.

Chimney Pot

Ornate terra-cotta chimney pots should not be overlooked as attractive and interesting plant containers. They look a little self-conscious and

awkward if displayed alone, but one is effective as the focal point of a large group, or placed in a mixed border where the plants can grow around it.

Materials

A chimney pot • Crockery shards • Peat- or soil-based potting soil

The Plants

Trailing plants and ground-cover roses are good choices for chimney pots because the plants will cover the stark body but leave the more interesting top exposed. Climbers are a good choice, but most would be too large for such a small amount of soil. However, the smaller clematis is a perfect choice.

1 Clematis "Helsingborg"

1. The size of the chimney pot is not important. Place crockery shards in the bottom, and fill with soil to the base of the castellations. Here, a terra-cotta copy has been used. For real chimney pots, place a suitable plastic flowerpot in the bottom of the container to act as a base. If the chimney pot is tall, partially fill with rubble to reduce the amount of compost required.

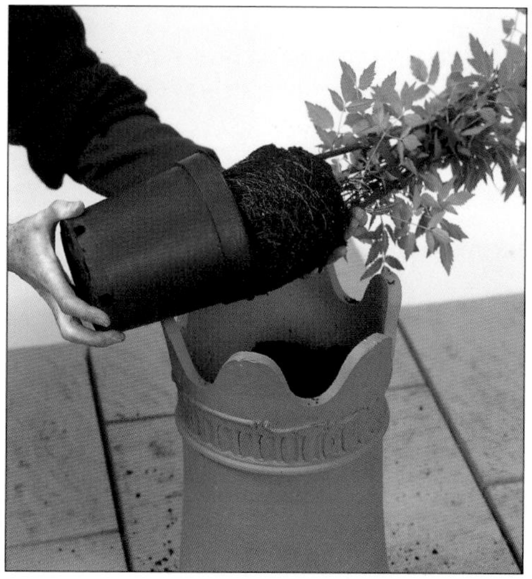

2. Remove the clematis from the flowerpot by inverting it, squeezing the sides, and gently easing out the rootball. Tease out the roots before planting.

3. Clematis should be planted at least 8 inches lower than the top of the rootball, so it will rejuvenate from below the surface if attacked by clematis wilt, an airborne fungus, which can otherwise kill young plants. Add potting soil to bring the level up to 2½ inches below the base of the castellation.

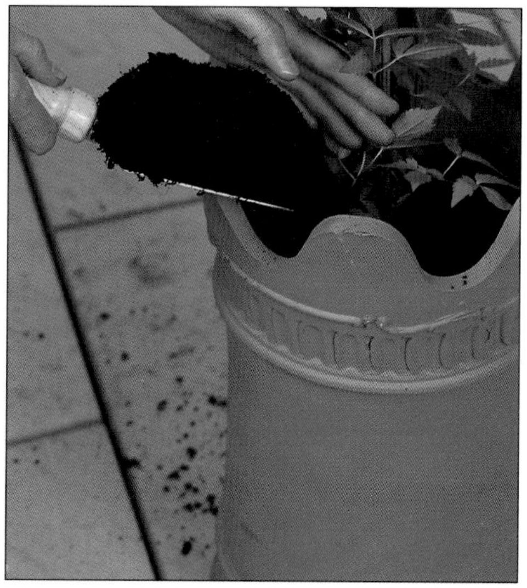

4. Untie the plant from the supporting cane to allow it to cascade over the edge of the container.

QUICK TIPS

Planting time: early spring
Light: sun or shade

Care: feed with a liquid fertilizer in April to encourage flowering, and then feed monthly throughout the summer only. Do not neglect the watering during the summer when it is not in flower. It will require watering each day during hot weather, like any other container.
Life expectancy: even small clematis have a limited life in a small container. Replace after three years.

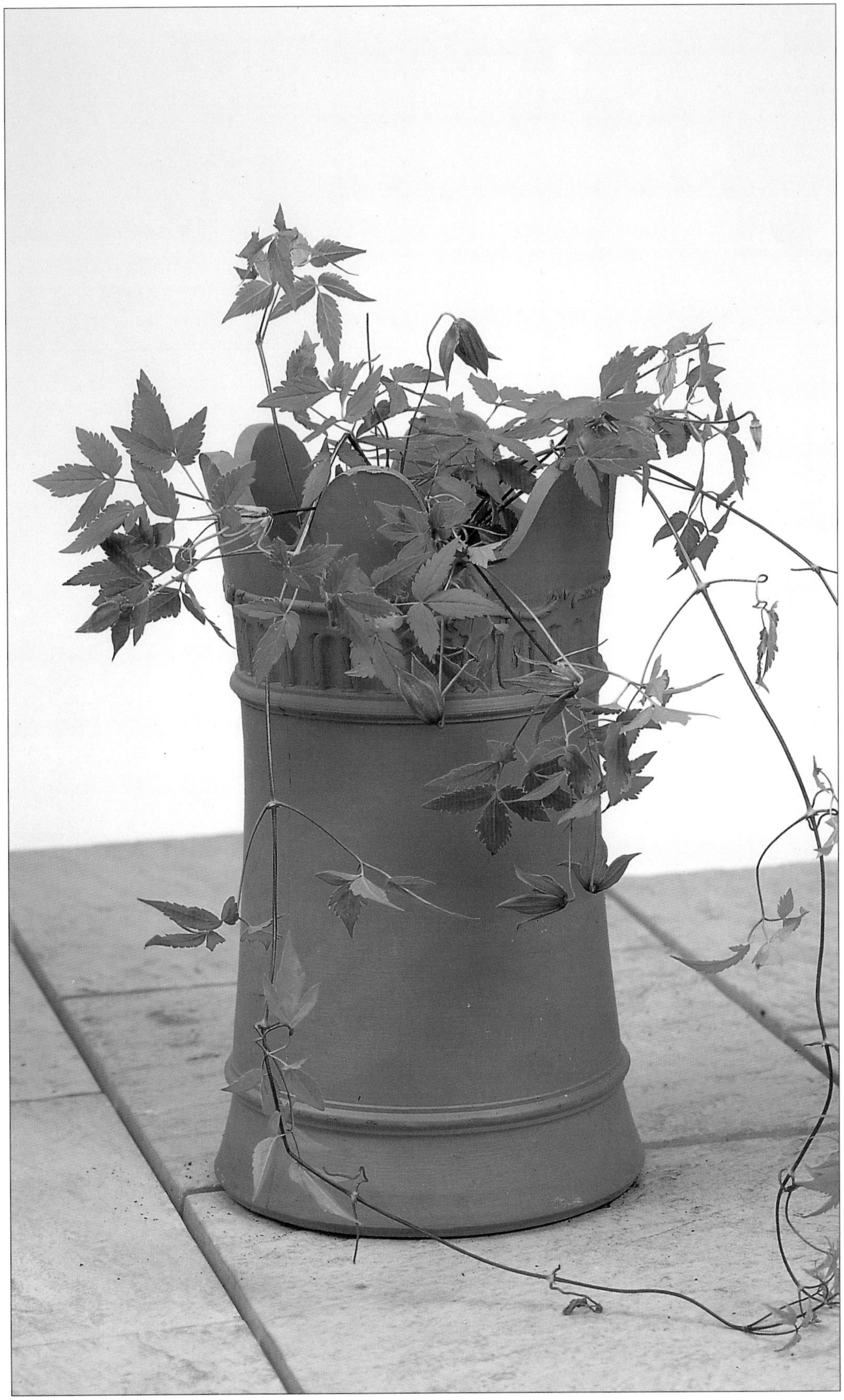

5. If the chimney pot is small, like this one, place it on a plinth, or on top of a low wall, to allow the climber room to develop.

Circular Group For Sun

Containers dotted randomly around the flower garden are not being used to their best advantage. Simply placing them together in a group is instantly more attractive. The easiest changes

in a garden are often the most effective, such as the grouping of one large, one medium, and one small container in decreasing circles. Urns can often look good even without plants.

Materials

Five mixed-size containers • a large container, 11inches in diameter • Crockery shards • Peat-based potting soil

1. Placing containers in rows is a common way to display them. This semicircular group is most effective on the top of a wall, or on a large windowsill. On a patio, it may be less effective because it may form a barrier.

2. The pink and red zonal geraniums, the *Campanula* "G. F. Wilson," and the *Helichrysum petiolare* look better pulled together into a group, but still lack a focal point and height.

3 zonal geraniums, 2 red and 1 pink

1 Helichrysum petiolare

The Plants

Strong, bright colors in patio container plants are important when the sun is high. The campanula bears clusters of lavender or pale blue flowers in summer, which provide contrast to the striking geraniums. The group is further lifted by the softness of the helichrysum. The New Zealand cabbage palm suggests a cooling fountain. Spiky plants create interesting effects when their shadows come in to play.

1 Campanula "G. F. Wilson"

1 New Zealand cabbage palm (Cordyline australis)

3. A few spiky plants can make all the difference. Try adding groups of iris to an uninteresting mixed border. In this case, a New Zealand cabbage palm adds a central feature and sudden impact to a "flat" scheme.

QUICK TIPS

Planting time: spring **Light:** sun

Care: each morning check the soil for moisture, and only water if dry. The campanula may require two or three waterings daily in hot weather.
Life expectancy: All the plants used are perennials, and may remain in their containers for many years if kept in a frost-free environment.

DESERT PLANT GROUP

Well, perhaps not a desert, but certainly for a hot, dry sunroom or patio. The plants used are all sun-lovers, and will require protection from frost. This is

the perfect choice for a Spanish- or Mexican-style garden where the temperatures are very high, there is little water, and few plants will grow.

Materials

Five terra-cotta pots, one each of 10 inches diameter x 7 inches high; 7½ inches diameter x 7 inches high; 7½ inches x 6 inches; and two 8 inches x 4 inches dishes • Crockery shards • Soil-based potting compost • Sharp gravel

QUICK TIPS

Planting time: at any time of the year
Light: full sun

Care: this scheme will tolerate neglect. In normal conditions, water once a week in summer, but not at all during the winter months.
Life expectancy: the plants can be kept in their containers for several years, and will only need attention if they outgrow their pots.

The Plants

This grouping of plants emphasizes the sharp outlines of the cacti family. The tiny white hairs that cover the houseleeks give the impression of a spider's web, contrasting with the bold, spiky mother-in-law's tongue. Echeveria, a low-growing succulent, will produce orange and yellow flowers in early summer, bringing a sprinkling of color to this unusual display.

1 mother-in-law's tongue (Sansevieria trifasciata)

1 agave (Agave americana "Variegata")

3 echeverias (Echeveria derenbergii)

1 cactus (Echinocactus grusonii)

5 cobweb houseleeks (Sempervivum arachnoideum)

1. Prepare each container by placing crockery shards over the drainage holes. Mix the sharp gravel with the soil, in the ratio 3 parts soil to 1 part gravel. Plant the largest container with the agave. This bold, spiky plant forms the centerpiece of the scheme. One of the two dishes is planted with the 3 echeverias, a low-growing succulent.

2. A globe-shaped cactus has been selected for the smallest container. Since the whole scheme lacks foliage and flowers, extremes in form have been chosen to add impact, and this globe shape contrasts well with the sword leaves of the agave.

AN ALTERNATIVE PLANTING

Plant a thread agave (*Agave filifera*) to replace the agave; a crassula (*Crassula socialis*) to replace the echeveria; an old lady cactus (*Mammillaria hahniana*) to replace the echinocactus; a pinwheel (*Aeonium haworthii*) to replace the houseleeks; and an organ pipe cactus (*Lemaireocereus marginatus*) to replace the mother-in-law's tongue.

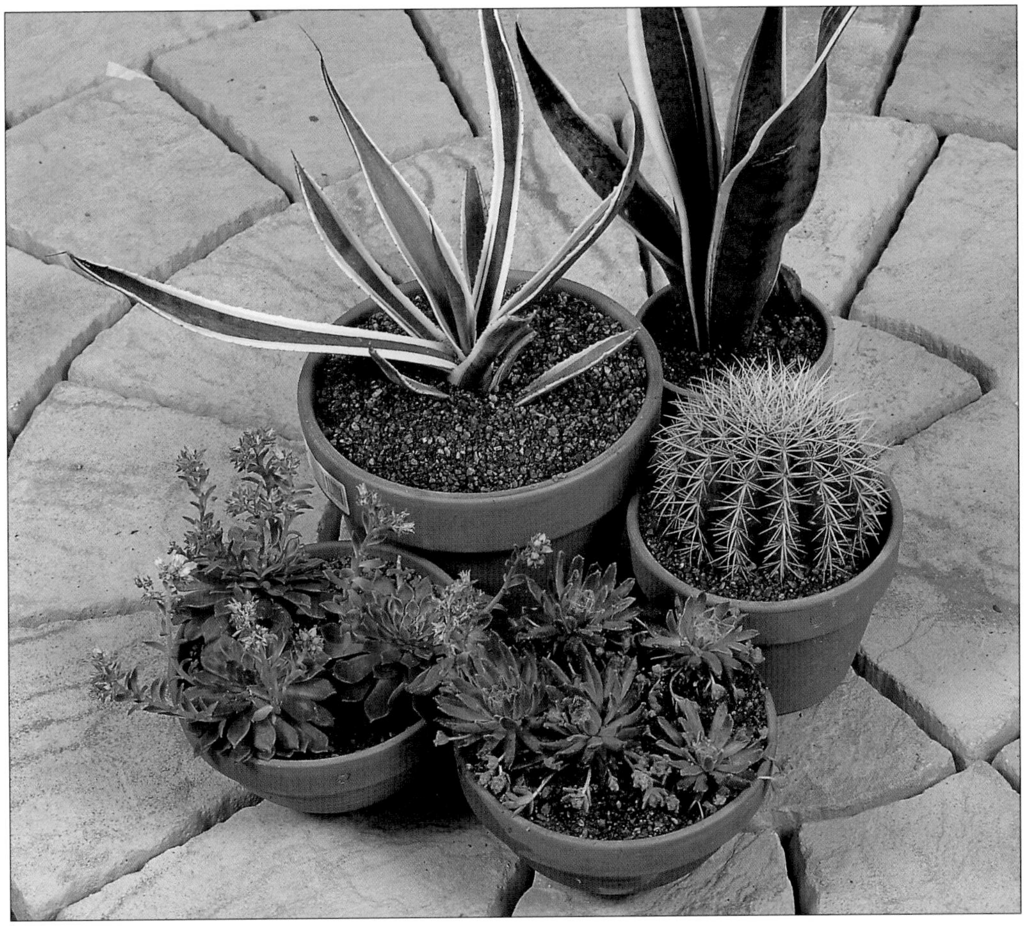

3. These three containers make a good display on their own, but you can go further. Plant up the second dish with the 5 cobweb houseleeks. Plant the mother-in-law's tongue in the final container to give an upright dimension to the arrangement.

SHADE GROUP

This grouping would be perfect on a shady patio or in a cool north- or east-facing sunroom. Many town gardens and roof gardens, which are shaded by trees and taller buildings,

have their whole planting scheme in containers. This grouping would be the perfect central feature in such a scheme. Try introducing a small upright statue into the group.

Materials

Five containers, one each of 20 inches diameter x 18 inches high; 16 inches x 12 inches high; 10 inches x 7½ inches; 12 inches x 9½ inches; 9 inches x 7 inches and 14 inches x 10 inches

QUICK TIPS

Planting time: at any time of the year
Light: partial or full shade

Care: it is essential that the soil in the containers is kept moist; although it is not necessary for all the plants, they will be much happier. It is best to use rainwater, because the pieris and the fetterbush prefer acid conditions.
Life expectancy: The bamboo, pieris, fetterbush, and baby's-tears will eventually outgrow their containers. Replanted into larger containers, they will be happy for an indefinite period. The hosta and astilbe will also outgrow their containers, but these can be divided and replanted.

The Plants

1 pieris (Pieris "Forest Flame"*)*

1 hosta (Hosta sieboldiana "Elegans"*)*

1 fetterbush (Leucothoe fontanesiana "Scarletta"*) Hanging, white pitcher-shaped flowers in spring*

1 baby's-tears (Soleirolia soleirolii, also known as Helxine soleirolii)
Tiny pale green leaves forming a mound

1 bamboo (Fargesia spathaceus, also known as Arundinaria murieliae)

1 astilbe (Astilbe "Peach Blossom"*)*

1. The main plant in the group is a bamboo. Bamboos are excellent subjects for dry or damp shade, and perfect in large containers.

2. The next two plants in the group are moisture-loving and must not be allowed to dry out. The lower of the two is baby's-tears, whose tiny pale green leaves form a mound. It is often sold as a houseplant, but is perfectly hardy in the right conditions (in the garden it grows where it wants to grow, not where you want it to!). The larger plant is an astilbe, which is normally found in damp soil beside a pool, the tall, feathery pink flowers in early summer and the fern-like leaves contrasting well with so many other plants.

3. Pieris, which has white flowers in spring followed by bright red new growth, requires an acid soil and is usually found in a woodland garden (use an ericaceous compost for acid-loving plants).

4. To finish off the scheme, a fetterbush which has hanging white pitcher-shaped flowers in spring, and a hosta have been selected. The fetterbush, like the pieris, requires an acid soil. Its shape, and that of the hosta, add solidity to the design.

SUMMER STRAWBERRY POT

Originally designed to grow strawberries, this terra-cotta container looks good planted with herbs beside the kitchen door, where they can be harvested for cooking.

In a mixed border, it adds height and extra interest, and a group of three strawberry pots of different sizes, planted with a mix of plants, makes an excellent and unusual focal point for a

Materials

A strawberry pot 15 inches x 6½ inches • Crockery shards • Peat-based or lightweight potting soil (so container is light to move)

QUICK TIPS

Planting time: spring **Light:** full sun

Care: bring into a frost-free environment during the winter, because the plants used are half-hardy perennials.
Life expectancy: usually one summer, but several years if protected from frost.

1. Place a generous layer of crockery shards in the bottom of the pot. This will help drainage and stop the soil from falling through the drainage holes in the bottom of the container.

2. Fill the container with a peat-based or lightweight potting soil to the lowest holes on the side of the pot.

The Plants

The lotus, its gray leaves sprawling over the sides of the pot, contrasts well with the terra-cotta container and the variegated leaves and pink flowers of the polygonum, of similar habit. The rich blue flowers of trailing lobelia and a variegated scented-leaf geranium with tiny pink flowers completes the arrangement.

2 Lotus berthelotii

4 polygonums
(Polygonum capitatum "Pink Bubbles"*)*

2 Lobelia "Kathleen Mallard"

1 scented-leaf geranium
(Pelargonium "Lady Plymouth"*)*

3. Collect together all the plants you intend to use before starting to plant.

4. Plant 2 polygonums and 2 *Lotus berthelotii* in the first layer. To remove a plant, invert the plastic pot and gently squeeze its sides. Tease out the roots, and prepare the plant for planting.

5. Using both hands, carefully insert the plant into the container.

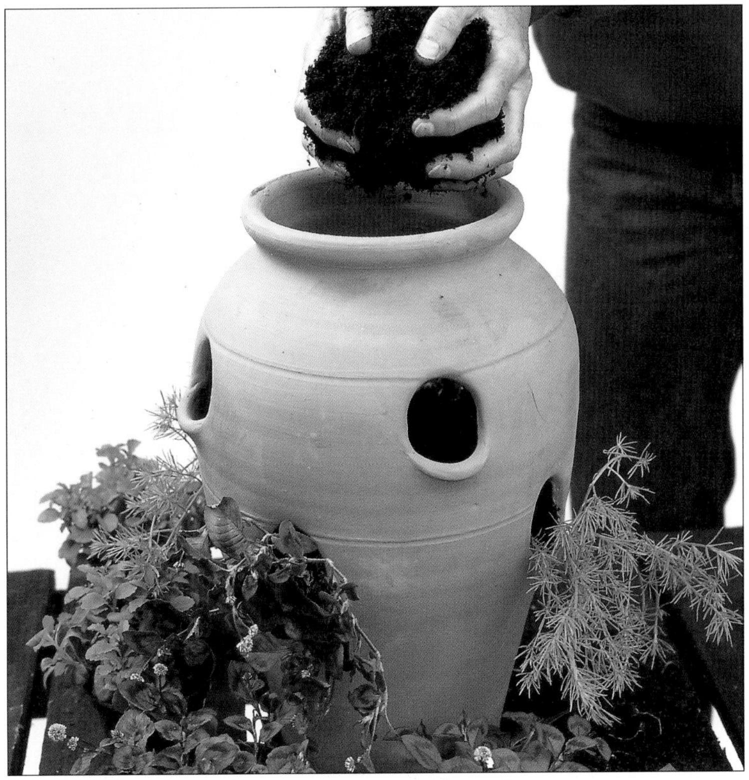

6. Add more potting soil, carefully consolidating it firmly around the plant roots. Bring the level up to the second layer of holes. Plant the next four plants: the 2 lobelia and 2 more polygonums.

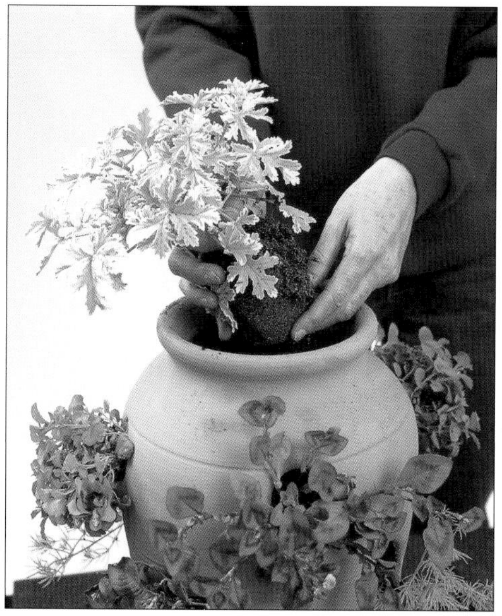

7. Finally, the arrangement is finished off with the scented-leaf geranium.

AN ALTERNATIVE PLANTING

For a smaller strawberry pot, 12inches x 7inches, plant 3 trailing lobelia *(Lobelia erinus pendula)* in the first layer of holes; 3 strawberry plants in the second layer; and finish off the container with a trailing fuchsia (*Fuchsia* "Cascade").

The strawberries can remain in the container for three or four years, but the lobelia will need replacing each spring. The fuchsia is a tender perennial and must be brought into a frost-free place during the winter.

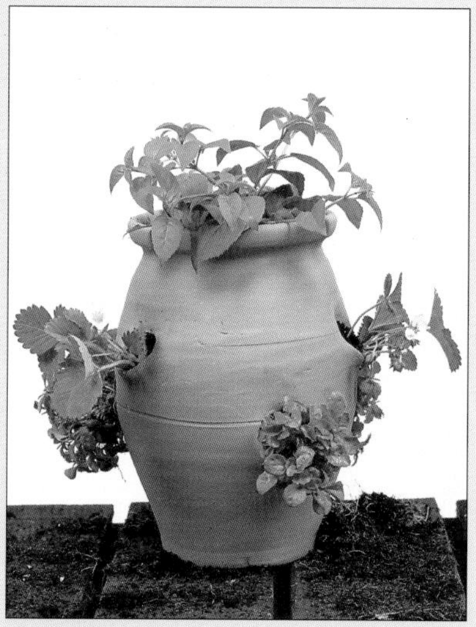

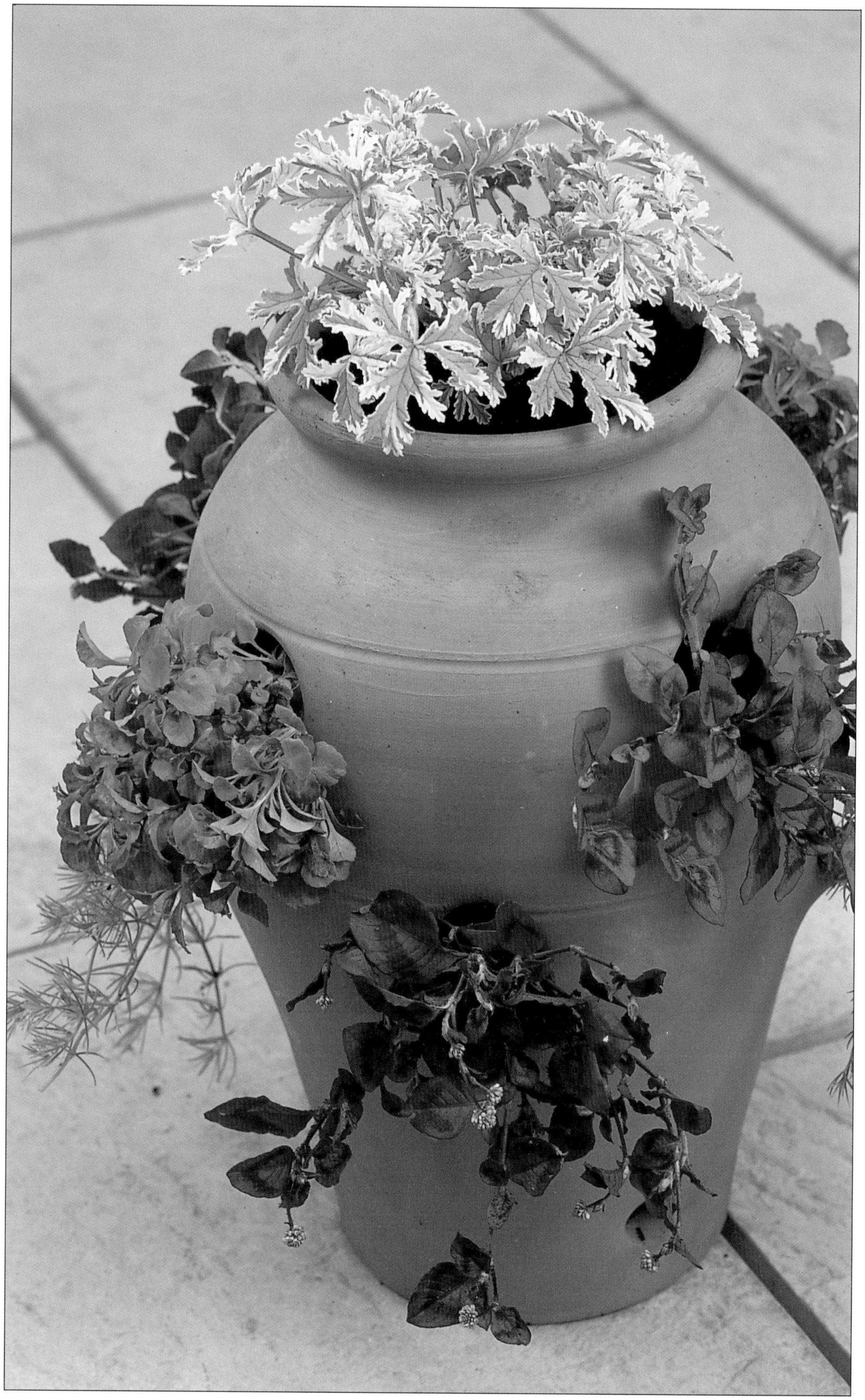

8. When planting is finished, water the container thoroughly.

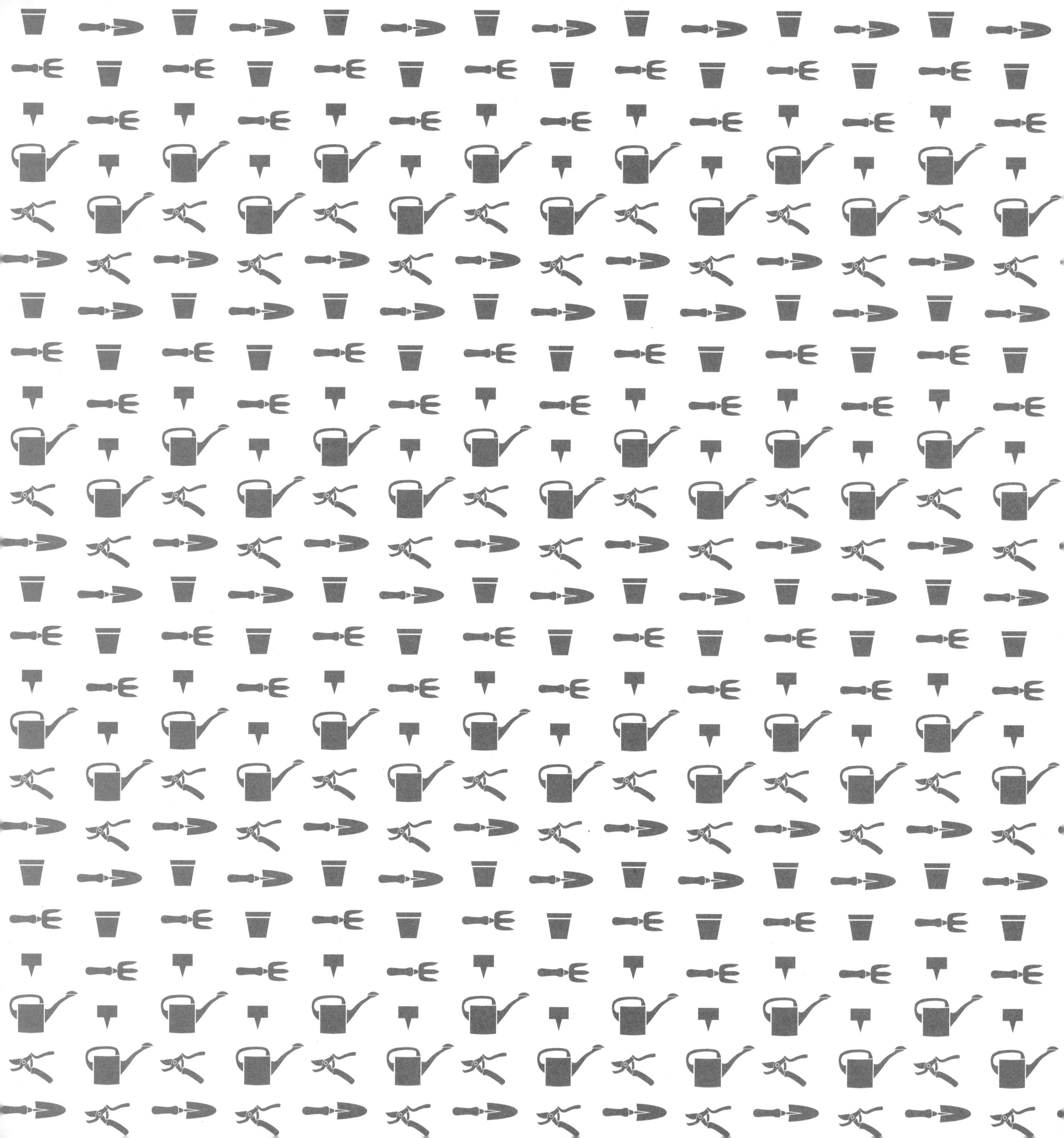